There's A Girl In My Soup

A Comedy

Terence Frisby

A Samuel French Acting Edition

SAMUELFRENCH-LONDON.CO.UK
SAMUELFRENCH.COM

Copyright © 1966 by Terence Frisby
All Rights Reserved

THERE'S A GIRL IN MY SOUP is fully protected under the copyright laws of the British Commonwealth, including Canada, the United States of America, and all other countries of the Copyright Union. All rights, including professional and amateur stage productions, recitation, lecturing, public reading, motion picture, radio broadcasting, television and the rights of translation into foreign languages are strictly reserved.

ISBN 978-0-573-01440-6

www.samuelfrench-london.co.uk

www.samuelfrench.com

FOR AMATEUR PRODUCTION ENQUIRIES

UNITED KINGDOM AND WORLD EXCLUDING NORTH AMERICA

plays@SamuelFrench-London.co.uk

020 7255 4302/01

Each title is subject to availability from Samuel French, depending upon country of performance.

CAUTION: Professional and amateur producers are hereby warned that *THERE'S A GIRL IN MY SOUP* is subject to a licensing fee. Publication of this play does not imply availability for performance. Both amateurs and professionals considering a production are strongly advised to apply to the appropriate agent before starting rehearsals, advertising, or booking a theatre. A licensing fee must be paid whether the title is presented for charity or gain and whether or not admission is charged.

The professional rights in this play are controlled by Lemon Unna & Durbridge, Summit House, 170 Finchley Road, London, NW3 6BP.

No one shall make any changes in this title for the purpose of production. No part of this book may be reproduced, stored in a retrieval system, or transmitted in any form, by any means, now known or yet to be invented, including mechanical, electronic, photocopying, recording, videotaping, or otherwise, without the prior written permission of the publisher. No one shall upload this title, or part of this title, to any social media websites.

The right of Terence Frisby to be identified as author of this work has been asserted by him in accordance with Section 77 of the Copyright, Designs and Patents Act 1988

THERE'S A GIRL IN MY SOUP

Produced by Michael Codron at the Globe Theatre, London, on the 15th June 1966, with the following cast of characters:

(in order of their appearance)

ROBERT DANVERS	Donald Sinden
CLARE DORLATON-FINCH	Jill Melford
ANDREW HUNTER	Jon Pertwee
PORTER	Anthony Sagar
PAOLA	Zeynep Tarimer
MARION	Barbara Ferris
JIMMY	Clive Francis

The play directed by ROBERT CHETWYN
Setting by HUTCHINSON SCOTT

SYNOPSIS OF SCENES

The action takes place in Robert Danvers's flat in London

ACT I
An evening in early summer

ACT II
The next morning

ACT III
Two weeks later

In each act the lights fade to denote the passing of a few hours

Time—the present

ACT I

SCENE—*Robert's flat. An evening in early summer.*
The flat is situated in S.W.3, and is superb. The set consists of the main room, kitchen, bedroom and outside corridor. Sliding screens divide the bedroom and kitchen from the living-room. The bedroom is L, *the hall and corridor are* R. *The kitchen is up* C, *and between it and the living-room runs a large dividing unit. There is a spare room off* R.

When the CURTAIN *rises,* ROBERT *and* CLARE *are on the sofa embracing.* ROBERT *imagines himself to be the last word in charm and intelligence. In fact, he is conceited, vain and pompous—especially pompous. A peacock of a man, forever preening. The screens hiding the kitchen are closed, and the record-player is giving soft music.*

ROBERT. You feel like a tender spring chicken.
CLARE. Can't you forget your stomach for one moment?
ROBERT. Your lipstick has a very pleasant dry flavour that is brought out by your scent. There's the merest suggestion of something like tarragon.
CLARE. I'm so glad for you.
ROBERT. Don't sneer. A delicately roasted tarragon chicken is a joy.
CLARE. In a minute I'll lay an egg.

(ROBERT *bites her neck. She breaks away*)

Ow. I think you've taken a lump out of me. You'd better give up being a professional gourmet; it's obviously warping you.
ROBERT. Nonsense. Like any ordinary man, the way to even *my* heart is through my stomach. My God, but you're lovely.
CLARE. Oh, Robert, I do love you.
ROBERT. I know.
CLARE. And?
ROBERT. And?
CLARE. And.
ROBERT. And I adore you. Don't lose the place for a moment.

(ROBERT *goes into the bedroom, flicks the coverlet back off the bed, switches on the electric blanket, removes his jacket and his tie and comes back to the living-room. As* ROBERT *returns,* CLARE *notes his change*)

CLARE (*sliding to the* R *end of the sofa; casually*) By the way.
ROBERT. Hm?
CLARE. Guess what happened to me the day before yesterday.
ROBERT. What? (*He sits beside her and kisses the back of her neck*)

CLARE. Guess.
ROBERT. I have no idea. (*He eases off a shoe*)
CLARE. I had a proposal.
ROBERT (*kissing her back*) What was it?
CLARE. A proposal.
ROBERT. Yes, I heard—oh, you mean a *proposal*.
CLARE. Yes.
ROBERT. Poor chap. (*He removes his second shoe*)
CLARE. What?
ROBERT. Well, you obviously turned him down.
CLARE. Ah, That's where you're wrong.
ROBERT. You accepted him?
CLARE. No. I kept him on a low flame.
ROBERT. Very wise. (*Rising*) That blanket should be warm by now.

(ROBERT *bends to pick her up to carry her to the bedroom*)

CLARE (*crossing her legs to stop him*) Now guess when I've got to let him know definitely.
ROBERT. Darling, this is a lovely game, but shall we play it after.
CLARE. No, before. While you're still hungry.
ROBERT (*Sitting back in sofa*) I've no idea. When?
CLARE. I said I'd let him know tonight.
ROBERT. Tonight?
CLARE. Yes. (*Looking at him*) I knew I'd be seeing you this afternoon.

(ROBERT *realizes what she is getting at and moves away along the sofa*)

Well—should I?
ROBERT. Marry him, you mean?
CLARE. Yes.
ROBERT. Clare, really. I couldn't possibly interfere in your affairs.
CLARE. Well, you haven't been doing badly up till now. You see, he loves me, so naturally he wants to marry me.
ROBERT. Naturally.
CLARE. I mean, it is only natural for a man to want to marry the woman he loves.
ROBERT. Quite.
CLARE. You said just now that you loved me.
ROBERT. I did not.
CLARE. You said you adored me.
ROBERT. That's not quite the same thing, is it?
CLARE (*after a pause*) I see. (*She rises and picks up her coat*) Then I'd better marry him, hadn't I?
ROBERT. If you say so. (*Taking her coat from her*) Clare, darling Clare. Then this is our last time together. After six glorious months. Let's make it wonderful, memorable (*He puts her coat on the sofa, then puts his arms round her and moves her towards the bedroom*)

CLARE (*breaking away*) No, that's out. (*Lying across the back of the sofa*) Your option has expired.
ROBERT. Darling, wouldn't it be better to end with a bang rather than a whimper?
CLARE (*primly*) No. It wouldn't be fair to him. He has strong moral views about personal relationships.
ROBERT. I'm sure you'll make him very happy. (*Going into the hall*) My God, is that the time? I had no idea. I'll get the porter to get you a taxi. How time flies when I'm with you, Clare. (*On the house phone*) Oh, John, get me a taxi, would you? Quickly . . . Then come up . . . Thank you. (*He rings off, then turns off the record-player*) Perhaps we could meet next week.
CLARE (*sitting up*) You only want me for one thing.
ROBERT. Yes, but what a lovely thing.

(CLARE *laughs, in spite of herself*)

My God, but you're lovely. (*Putting his arms round her*) Oh, Clare, we've had such fun. Let's keep it like this, right till the end.
CLARE. This is the end.
ROBERT. Then what about a closing ceremony?
CLARE. Oh, Robert, you're impossible. (*She laughs*)
ROBERT. I know.

(ROBERT *picks her up and carries her to the bedroom.* ANDREW *enters the corridor. He looks very harassed.* ROBERT *puts Clare on the bed and is about to join her when* ANDREW *rings the bell, and mops his brow*)

Hell's nostrils! Who's that?
CLARE. It's my taxi.
ROBERT. Oh, yes. I'll tell him to come back in half an hour.
CLARE. My God, at least make it forty-five minutes.

(ROBERT *goes to the door extracting a note from his pocket.* CLARE *kicks her shoes off and goes into the bathroom with her bag.* ROBERT *opens the door*)

ROBERT. Thank you, John, but I won't be needing . . . Andrew!
ANDREW. Hallo, old boy.
ROBERT. What the hell are you doing here?
ANDREW. Now, don't you start. I've had a basinful for one afternoon.
ROBERT. Andrew, it's a shade awkward at the moment . . .
ANDREW. Why? Have you got some concoction on the boil?
ROBERT. No.
ANDREW. Working on a new dish?
ROBERT. No.
ANDREW. Writing a recipe?
ROBERT. No.
ANDREW. Then why the hell aren't you ready?

ROBERT. Ready for what?
ANDREW. I'm picking you up.
ROBERT. Yes. Tomorrow.
ANDREW. No. Today.
ROBERT. No, tomorrow. Friday.
ANDREW. Today is Friday.
ROBERT. Is it?
ANDREW. Yes.
ROBERT. Whatever happened to Thursday?
ANDREW (*entering the room*) Come on. Hurry up. We're waiting.
ROBERT. We? Is Gilly with you?
ANDREW. Yes. And the kids.
ROBERT (*closing the hall door*) The kids. Where are they?
ANDREW. Don't worry. (*Moving to the drinks*) They're downstairs, shackled into the car. Can I have a drink? (*He pours himself a drink*) I need one. Gilly decided to call for me at the office, with the five kids, the new au pair and the dog. Phew! The tortoise and the goldfish decided to stay at home, which was pretty sensible of them.
ROBERT. I'm afraid I can't come just at this moment.
ANDREW. Can't? You've got to. I'm not facing that screaming mob without Uncle Robert.
ROBERT. You'll have to.
ANDREW. Why?

(CLARE *enters the bedroom, undressed and holding a bathrobe in front of her*)

CLARE (*calling*) Robert, darling.

(ANDREW *stares at the bedroom, then at his watch*)

ANDREW. Five-thirty. It's in the middle of the rush hour.
CLARE. Darling.
ROBERT. Coming, darling.
CLARE. Yes, well, do. (*She goes back into the bathroom*)
ANDREW. Are you working 'em in shifts now?
ROBERT. I'm sorry, old boy, I'll have to join you in Putney later.
ANDREW. Robert now. You've promised my kids you'd read 'em bed time stories. You can't disappoint them.
ROBERT. Oh, yes, I can.
ANDREW. Now, listen. Either you come back with me, or I let them loose up here.
ROBERT. What?
ANDREW. Take your pick.
ROBERT. That's a filthy trick.
ANDREW (*sitting in the chair* R) This is a filthy situation.

(ROBERT *and* ANDREW *glare at each other.* CLARE *enters the bedroom, now clad in the bathrobe*)

CLARE (*irritably*) Darling. Are you coming? (*She lies on the bed*)

ANDREW. And see how she enjoys it with five healthily curious children for company.
ROBERT (*quietly*) All right, then. You'll have to help.
ANDREW. Help?
ROBERT (*moving to the bedroom*) Help get rid of her.
ANDREW. Oh.
CLARE. Darling, where are you?

(ROBERT *enters the bedroom*)

ROBERT. Darling, there's an idiot friend of mine here I can't get rid of. I have to go out. I'm terribly sorry.
CLARE. I have just taken off my lipstick. You are the bottom.

(CLARE *slams off into the bathroom.* JOHN *enters the corridor and rings the bell*)

ROBERT (*calling to Andrew*) There's John. Let him in, will you? She won't make a scene in front of the porter.
ANDREW. Oh, good.

(ANDREW *opens the hall door.* ROBERT *exits to bathroom*)

Hallo, John. Come on in. (*He moves back into the room*)
JOHN (*entering the room*) Afternoon, Mr Hunter. Mr Danvers's taxi is waiting.
ANDREW. They won't be long. (*He sits on the divider*)
JOHN. And Mrs Hunter asked me to tell you to get a move on before she murdered one of the kids.
ANDREW. Right.
JOHN. Quite a little crowd you got now. All thriving, I hope.
ANDREW. Yes, bursting with energy. Cigarette?
JOHN. Oh, ta. He got something for me to carry, has he?
ANDREW. No, I think he just—um . . .
JOHN. Wanted me to wait.
ANDREW. More or less, yes.
JOHN. Oh. Shame. (*He closes the hall door*) She only came in half an hour ago, too.
ANDREW. Hm?
JOHN. Didn't expect no signs of life just yet.
ANDREW. Ah.
JOHN. I've often had to hang about, you know. Sort of—referee.
ANDREW. Really?
JOHN. Yes, I don't get it. They go out of here miserable, crying, hysterical, threatening suicide. I mean, I know he cooks every week on telly, but he's not that fantastic.
ANDREW. No.
JOHN. And they're all marvellous-looking, too. All Grade A pasteurized, full cream. Nothing over the top for him. Nothing off., Oh, no. How's Mrs Hunter, by the way?

ANDREW. Eh? Oh, very fit, thank you very much.
JOHN. Look at this one, eh? Goh! She's lovely, isn't she?
ANDREW. Well, I haven't really seen her yet.
JOHN. Oh, dear. Marvellous, she is. Lovely legs on her.
ANDREW. Yes?
JOHN. They're-er—what's the right word?—um—they're very leggy legs, if you see what I mean.
ANDREW. I think so. Yes.
JOHN. And long, whawh, right up to her bum.
ANDREW. Really.
JOHN. Not like my old woman. Her arse comes down to meet her knees.

(ROBERT *enters from the bathroom and opens the bedroom screens*)

ROBERT. All's well. Ah, John, no need for you to wait. Tell the taxi driver the lady's just coming.
JOHN (*moving to the hall*) Right, sir.

(JOHN *exits down the corridor*. CLARE *enters from the bathroom, looking in a hand-mirror*)

CLARE. Oh God, what a mess! (*She throws the mirror on the bed*)
ROBERT. Perfection, darling, perfection.
CLARE. Hm.
ROBERT. Ah, Andrew. I'd like you to meet Miss Dorlaton-Finch. Clare, this is Andrew Hunter. He's the editor of the magazine I do a weekly column for.

(ANDREW *and* CLARE *shake hands and mutter greetings*)

Miss Dorlaton-Finch is just off, Andrew. (*He goes to the hall*)
ANDREW. Oh. What a shame.
CLARE. Yes, well, lovely meeting you. (*Moving to the hall*) Good-bye Mr—ah.
ANDREW. Good-bye, Miss—um.
ROBERT. Good-bye, darling Clare.
CLARE. *Au revoir*, you horrible man.
ROBERT. I'm sure you'll both be deeply happy.
CLARE. I'll send you an invitation to the wedding and don't turn up with a toast-rack and a Robert Danvers cookbook.
ROBERT. May I kiss the bride? (*He kisses Clare*) I'll ring you after the honeymoon.
CLARE. Do that.

(CLARE *exits*. ROBERT *comes into the room*)

ANDREW (*sitting in the chair* L) What a slob you are. You treat your sex life like a continuous wine tasting—roll 'em round and spit 'em out.

ROBERT (*picking up his shoes and moving to the bedroom*) After these blasted bedtime stories you're dragging me off to a party, aren't you? (*He collects his suit, shirt, socks and shoes from the dressing room*)
ANDREW. Yes.
ROBERT. Top up your drink while I change. (*He comes back into the room*) Where is this party?

(ROBERT *changes during the following scene*)

ANDREW (*pouring himself another drink*) Back here. Round the corner off the Kings Road somewhere.
ROBERT. Hell's eyebrows. (*Changing his shirt*) And you're dragging me all the way out to Putney just to read bedtime stories.
ANDREW. You never know, you might even enjoy yourself. Babar the Elephant gets pretty saucy in places. Anyway, it's time you gave all this philandering up, Robert. (*Moving* L) How old are you now? Forty what?
ROBERT. About that, yes.
ANDREW. You won't last. You'll snuff it prematurely one day, like that. (*He snaps his fingers*) Stiff as a board, leaving some female to dispose of your rotting corpse.

(*He sits on the* L *arm of the sofa*)

ROBERT. That's better than dying of a hag-ridden old age, leaving some female to dispose of your life insurance.
ANDREW. It's a funny thing, but all you womanizers seem to despise women.
ROBERT. Despise them? My dear fellow, the sight of a new, beautiful woman and the challenge she presents is—oh, better than being confronted with all the great dishes of the world cooked by all the chefs in history.
ANDREW (*putting his glass on the coffee-table*) Have you ever tried making friends with one?
ROBERT. Friends? You don't make friends with a roast duck, you eat it.

(ANDREW *takes out some papers*)

ANDREW. You must put that into one of your columns and see how your lady readers enjoy it. Here. These are for you.
ROBERT (*putting on his socks*) What's that?
ANDREW. Your air ticket to Lyons, your pass into the *foire des vins* at Mâcon, and your timetable for the week.
ROBERT. Thank you.
ANDREW. After the wine tastings we want a staff reporter to interview you.
ROBERT. Oh?
ANDREW. Over a slap-up meal, of course.
ROBERT. I'm all for that.

ANDREW. Quite. Oh, and we'll need a new photograph of you.
ROBERT (*putting his keys on the coffee-table*) Another one. What for?
ANDREW. For the cover of the Robert Danvers wines and foods edition.
ROBERT. You are putting one on the cover, then.
ANDREW. Yes, in glorious technicolor (*He puts the air ticket on the divider*) After all, you are the sexiest gourmet in the business.
ROBERT. Quite.

(ROBERT *removes his trousers*)

ANDREW. I say, they're very sharp knickers. Do they cost much?
ROBERT. I don't know. They were a present. Part of a set (*He puts on his other trousers*)
ANDREW. Ah, of course. Are they part of the great seductive image, too?
ROBERT. Not really. By the time you get to this stage you're home and dry.

(PAOLA *enters the corridor*)

ANDREW. Huh. And people say that women are emancipated.

(PAOLA *rings the doorbell*)

My God, Gilly. (*Moving* R) She'll be out of her mind. (*He goes to the door and opens it*)

(ROBERT *closes the bedroom screens*)

PAOLA. Sorry, Mr Hunter. Mrs Hunter says could you come, please, at once. The children are being . . .
ANDREW. Yes, yes. Come in. (*Moving* L) Hey, Robert, how long are you going to be? Gilly wants to know.
ROBERT. Ah, Gilly. Hallo. (*He puts his head round the screen*) Just changing into my best bib and—oh. (*He stares*)
PAOLA. How do you do. The children ask, when will you come, Mr Danvers.
ROBERT. Hm?
ANDREW. This is our new au pair, Paola. She's Italian and of a very good family.
ROBERT. Yes, I can see that. I'll be with you in a moment. Do sit down. Andrew, see that Miss—Paola gets a drink, would you. (*He returns to the bedroom*)

(PAOLA *goes to sit on the sofa*)

ANDREW. No. No drinks. Go and tell my wife that we're coming right now, would you?
PAOLA. Yes, Mr Hunter.
ANDREW (*Ushering Paola to the hall*) Off you go, then. Vite. Schnell. Mush. Whatever it is.

(ROBERT *checks himself in the mirror Clare threw onto the bed, then puts it on the bedside table* R)

ACT I THERE'S A GIRL IN MY SOUP

PAOLA. Yes, Mr Hunter.

(PAOLA *exits* R, *leaving the door open*. ROBERT *opens the screens*)

ROBERT. Well now. Is he taking good care of . . . Where is she?
ANDREW. I sent her back.
ROBERT. What did you do that for?
ANDREW (*sitting on the* R *arm of the sofa*) Don't worry. You'll see her downstairs. She won't have aged much.
ROBERT. My dear fellow, she's gorgeous, isn't she?
ANDREW. Hm? Yes, I suppose so.
ROBERT (*doing up his tie*) You can't wander about like that—just indifferent.

(ANDREW *shrugs*)

I now know why married men live longer. They're half-dead already.
ANDREW. Look here, I can appreciate a girl's looks just as well as you, without actually lathering up.

(ROBERT *laughs*)

ROBERT (*picking up his keys*) I suppose indifference is the prelude to incapability.
ANDREW. What?
ROBERT. Of course, that's why you've been breeding so busily. Your final flurry of fecundity before . . . (*He puts his thumbs down and makes a death rattle*)
ANDREW (*deeply offended*) And what about you? The great connoisseur of wine, women and two veg. If you didn't nip off to that health farm in Hampshire every five minutes to have your flue raked out, you'd have clinkered up years ago.
ROBERT. Hark who's talking. Your wick could do with a trim.
ANDREW. And as for your pipes. (*Rising*) How the blood gets through them, God knows. And you're flabby.
ROBERT (*putting on his socks*) Ha. That's solid muscle.
ANDREW. That is fat.
ROBERT. You're practically scraggy.
ANDREW. Scraggy? I'm in the peak of condition.
ROBERT (*putting on his shoes*) A fiver says I'm fitter.
ANDREW. Only five? Ha. I'll take you on any time you like.
ROBERT. Here and now.
ANDREW. Right.
ROBERT (*maliciously*) Your wife's waiting.
ANDREW. Blast my wife. Now, what shall we do for a trial? I know, press-ups.
ROBERT. You mean, like . . . (*He makes an arm movement*)
ANDREW. That is exactly what I mean. Huh. This'll be the easiest fiver I've ever earned in my life.

(*They move the coffee-table a little upstage*)

ROBERT. Ha. We'll make it ten, if you feel like that.

(*They put their fivers on the coffee-table*)

ANDREW (*airily*) No, no. I don't want to take advantage.
ROBERT. Windy.

(*They take off their jackets and put them on the sofa*)

ANDREW (*moving* RC) Right. We keep even time. The first one to flag or drop out loses. Right? (*He claps*)
ROBERT (*claps*) Right.

(*They both start to cool down and get worried. They clap once more each, then stand irresolutely*)

ANDREW. What are you waiting for?
ROBERT. You.
ANDREW. I'm ready.
ROBERT (*moving up* LC) Right.
ANDREW. Right.

(*They kneel;* ROBERT *behind the sofa*)

Oi. Come on, over here, facing each other, where I can keep an eye on you. Ready?

(ROBERT *moves below the sofa, facing Andrew*)

ROBERT. Ready.
ANDREW. Steady?
ROBERT. Steady.
ANDREW. Go.

(*They do two press-ups, counting.* ANDREW *barely moves. They get to about five.* ROBERT *is resting his knees on the floor.* ANDREW *has his bottom sticking up*)

Get your knees off the floor.
ROBERT. Get your arse off the ceiling.

(ANDREW *is in by far the worse state.* PAOLA *enters and stands by the door for a moment, nonplussed*)

PAOLA. Er—Mr Hunter. Excuse, but—Mr Hunter. (*She taps Andrew on the bottom*)
ANDREW. Ah! (*He collapses*)
ROBERT. I win. (*He hauls himself to his feet*)
ANDREW. Foul—I was interfered with.
PAOLA. Mrs Hunter has much anger, Mr Hunter.

(ANDREW *tries to speak, but can't. Very exhausted, he picks up the money and gives Robert his fiver*)

ANDREW. It's—it—it's a draw.
ROBERT. *A draw?*
ANDREW (*picking up his jacket and moving to the hall*) Match abandoned.
ROBERT. Here and now. We agreed.
ANDREW. I—Gilly—my wife—she's down—wait . . . She . . . Come on Pao—la—oh . . .

(ANDREW *staggers out, unable to get his breath.* PAOLA *makes to follow*)

ROBERT. Just a minute, Paola. Would you please give me a hand to move this? (*Lingering over the name*) Paola. What a lovely name.
PAOLA. Thank you.

(PAOLA *and* ROBERT *move the coffee-table back into position*)

ROBERT. Tell me. Do you speak English?
PAOLA. A small.
ROBERT. How very clever of you.
PAOLA. Thank you.
ROBERT. Do you like Chinese food?
PAOLA. Si. A lot.
ROBERT (*giving her his card*) My phone number. It would be indiscreet for me to phone you at their house.
PAOLA. So?
ROBERT. If you phone me at this number, we will eat the most wonderful Chinese meal—together.
PAOLA. Oh?
ROBERT. And afterwards—who knows?
PAOLA. That sounds very nice.
ROBERT. My God, but you're lovely.
PAOLA (*smiling*) Thank you.

(*They move to the hall*)

ROBERT. Have you been in England long?
PAOLA. A week.
ROBERT. A week. But you can't have seen anything yet. I must show you—

(ROBERT *and* PAOLA *exit* R. *The* LIGHTS *fade to a Black-out.*

After a pause, the LIGHTS *come up in the corridor.* ROBERT *and* MARION *enter. He unlocks the door into the room and lets them in, turning on the sitting-room lights*)

ROBERT. Here we are. Let me take your things.

(MARION *ignores him and goes into the sitting-room. She looks at her watch and checks it with a clock on the divider. He looks at himself briefly in the hall mirror, then follows her in. He turns on the record-player. She*

looks round. She sees him watching her, smiles briefly and continues to look round the room with detached curiosity. Not surprised or impressed.
ROBERT, *while remaining scrupulously polite, has a contained excitement that comes from being fairly certain he is about to have a new, attractive woman*)

Do you approve?

(MARION *shrugs*)

(*Smugly*) It's very comfortable.

(MARION *glances at him, taking in his attitude*)

Drink?

(*She nods*)

What would you like?
MARION. There's a choice, of course.
ROBERT. Of course.

(MARION *snorts loudly at some private joke. A long snoring sound*)

MARION. A big one?
ROBERT. Reasonable. Sherry, brandy, whisky, Scotch or rye; a few liqueurs; vodka, dubonnet, campari, slivovitz, port, saki, ouzo; or we could split a bottle of champagne or some other wine if you like. Well?
MARION. Got any beer?
ROBERT. No, but there's some meths in the cleaning cupboard if you care for it.
MARION. I'll have a bit of everything.
ROBERT (*smiling*) Are you trying to be difficult?
MARION. Yes.
ROBERT. It's not a mixture I recommend.
MARION. No. But can I have it?
ROBERT. If you really want to.

(*She snorts again*)

MARION. Whisky. (*She starts to take off her coat*)
ROBERT. Soda, or water?
MARION. Nothing.
ROBERT. Let me take your coat.
MARION (*suddenly eager*) No, I will. Where? (*Running to the hall*) Out here?
ROBERT. Yes. In that cupboard.

(MARION *hangs her coat in the hall cupboard. He stares at her, surprised at her sudden vitality. She stares back at him. He pours a drink*)

MARION. Oh, I will have some water.

ACT I   THERE'S A GIRL IN MY SOUP

(ROBERT *goes to the kitchen.* MARION *goes into the hall, looking for something. She can't find it, and as quietly as she can she opens the front door of the flat. She looks at the outside of the door and the wall beside it.* ROBERT *returns from the kitchen*)

ROBERT. Are you all right?

(*She jumps, and comes in*)

Is anything wrong?
MARION. No.
ROBERT. Were you leaving?
MARION. Just larking about.
ROBERT. Please do, if you wish
MARION. What?
ROBERT. Leave.
MARION. Do you want me to?
ROBERT. No, of course not.

(*She considers, then closes the door and puts her bag on the chair* RC)

Say when.

(*He is about to pour, but she takes the whisky before he can put any water in, then crosses* L)

MARION. You must be loaded.
ROBERT. Hm?
MARION (*looking round*) Well.
ROBERT. I am what I believe is described as comfortably off.
MARION (*giving the snort again*) I'll bet it is. (*She drinks her whisky at one gulp*) Cheers.
ROBERT. Do sit down. (*He indicates the chair* L, *then pours himself a whisky*)

(*She deliberately selects the sofa* R, *leaving room for him. He considers, then he sits down* L, *facing her. She notes this and looks at her watch. He looks at his, puzzled*)

That was quite a party, wasn't it?

(*She shrugs*)

Do you go to many like that?
MARION. Do you?
ROBERT. No. I'd hate to live next door to that crowd. What a racket?

(*She grunts non-commitally*)

You could hear that drummer half-way down the street.
MARION (*all at a rush*) He's not very good.
ROBERT. No, I didn't think he . . .
MARION. Too exhibitionist. He's been playing one-night stands with pop groups, and it's gone to his head a bit.

ROBERT. I see . . .
MARION. Anyway, he's really only a lino-layer.
ROBERT. Ah—
MARION. He used to be better. Could I have another one, please?
ROBERT (*putting his glass on the floor and rising*) Of course. (*He takes her glass*)

(*She takes a cigarette from the coffee-table*)

MARION. Can I have a cigarette?
ROBERT. I'm terribly sorry. I should have given you one. It was the business with the door.

(*He lights it for her*)

Were you leaving just now?
MARION. Did you think I was?
ROBERT (*moving to the drinks*) I wasn't sure.
MARION. I was looking for your name on the door. Or a letter to you.
ROBERT. Oh? What for?
MARION. To keep one up on you for a bit longer.
ROBERT. To *keep* one up on me?
MARION. By finding out your name.
ROBERT (*not understanding*) Ah. You mean you don't know my name?
MARION. No.
ROBERT. Nor who I am?
MARION. Should I?
ROBERT (*moving R of her with her drink*) It's just that I was under the impression that you did know when you came with me.
MARION. What is it, then?
ROBERT (*smugly*) I am Robert Danvers. (*He expects a reaction*)
MARION. Oh, that's nice for you. Who am I?
ROBERT. I've no idea.
MARION. See?
ROBERT (*moving above the sofa to L of it*) It wasn't that sort of party. We weren't exactly formally introduced. No one banged on the floor when I entered and said "Robert Danvers".

(*She still does not react*)

No one would have heard anyway, I suppose. What is your name?
MARION. Marion.
ROBERT. What a lovely name.
MARION. What?
ROBERT. Marion. It's a beautiful name.

(*She looks at him as if he's out of his mind, then looks at her watch. He does the same with his, puzzled*)

You didn't seem to be with anyone in particular. Were you?

MARION. Getting round, was I?
ROBERT. Sort of.
MARION. Till you picked me up.
ROBERT. Now wait a minute. When a strange girl comes up to me at a strange party and says: "How far away do you live?" and I say: "Ten minutes' walk or two minutes by taxi" and she says: "We'll take a taxi", I don't call that picking her up.
MARION. I noticed when I asked where you lived you didn't say where; you described how to get there.
ROBERT. A figure of speech.
MARION (*snorting again*) I'll bet you couldn't believe your luck,—kerplonk—right in your lap. Could I have another one, please? (*She holds out her glass*)
ROBERT. Are you trying to get tight?
MARION. Don't worry. It takes a lot more than this.
ROBERT (*rising and taking her glass to the drinks*) At least it's better for you than that stuff they were drinking at the party.
MARION. It was punch. Home-made.
ROBERT. From what, I wonder.
MARION. All the bottles that people brought, just emptied in, same as usual. Didn't you see it?
ROBERT. No. (*He hands her her drink*)
MARION. It was in the bath.
ROBERT. So that's what that was. (*Moves above the sofa then turns*) There was a girl paddling in it.
MARION. Yeah. I can't stand her. All mouth and trousers. Some pimply guardsman she'd picked up said he'd lick her feet dry if she paddled in it. Ergh. They're so show-offy, that sort.
ROBERT (*moving down* L) Oh, I don't know. As a gesture, it has a certain—savoir-faire.
MARION. Anyway, someone sat her down in it. That settled them both.
ROBERT. As you're obviously going to pour that stuff down you, would you care for something to eat?
MARION. Why, can you cook?
ROBERT. What would you like? Within reason.
MARION. I'll have a piece of bread.
ROBERT. Just bread?
MARION. Dry. To soak up this.

(ROBERT *goes to the kitchen*)

Can I turn this row off?
ROBERT. Don't you like it?
MARION (*rising*) Not much.
ROBERT. Were you alone?
MARION. What? (*She turns off the record-player*)
ROBERT. At the party?
MARION. Were you?

ROBERT. We're talking about you.
MARION. You are, you mean. I'm talking about you.

(ROBERT *returns from the kitchen, carrying the breadknife*)

ROBERT. So you are. No, I was with some friends. We got separated. I got into the wrong party by mistake.

(ROBERT *goes into the kitchen*)

MARION. Oh, yes, I didn't think of that. I knew you didn't belong, but I thought someone must have brought you. Some of those girls get the oddest fellers.

(ROBERT *returns with a piece of bread on a plate*)

ROBERT. I would have thought I was the only normal one there.
MARION. Depends on your idea of normality, doesn't it?
ROBERT. Yes, I suppose it does. We had the right house, but the wrong flat. Your do was in the basement, ours was up on top.
MARION. But of course.
ROBERT (*giving Marion the bread*) Your bread.
MARION (*sitting* C *on the sofa*) Thank you. Slice off a cut loaf. Dead right.
ROBERT (*sitting on the* R *arm of the sofa*) Who were you with?
MARION. No one. Why?
ROBERT. Who invited you?
MARION. No one. Why?
ROBERT. I was just wondering about you.
MARION. Why?
ROBERT. I was interested.
MARION. In what?
ROBERT. Why do you always answer a question with a question?
MARION. Why do you?
ROBERT. Yes. Would you like another drink?
MARION. Are you trying to get me tight?
ROBERT (*rising and moving* L *above the sofa*) You're frightening enough sober.
MARION (*holding out her glass*) Yes, please.
ROBERT (*refilling her glass*) Were you with that chap who you were chatting with in the kitchen when I walked in?
MARION. Snogging with, you mean?
ROBERT. I suppose I do.
MARION. No. He just happened to be passing.
ROBERT. I thought you seemed to have lost him, when you came up to me later.
MARION. Well, I would have, wouldn't I?

(ROBERT *brings her drink, hands it to her and sits beside her on the sofa, relaxing easily.* MARION *looks at her watch. So does he*)

ROBERT. Mind you, in that party you could have lost Nelson's column. What was that dance they were all doing?
MARION. Which one?
ROBERT. I'm not sure. There was one where you stand still and just wobble. A girl stood in front of me doing it. I thought she'd dropped a lighted cigarette down and was trying to work it through.
MARION. Like this, you mean. (*She starts to demonstrate, sitting down*)
ROBERT. That's the one.
MARION. Oh. (*She spills some whisky on herself*)
ROBERT. Here. Quickly. Before it dries. (*He hands her his handkerchief*)

(*She sits still, offering her left shoulder. He wipes it, meticulously unsexy; concentrating on the job, while she stares at him. He finishes*)

There.

(*They remain close for a while, staring evenly at each other. Then he smiles and holds out his hand*)

Would you care for some more?
MARION (*giving him her glass*) Thank you.

(*He rises to refill it, chuckling to himself*)

What's funny?
ROBERT. Nothing. I thought the idea of going dancing was to get to know people. Not to stand on your own waving your limbs about.
MARION. The idea of going dancing is to dance. Waving your limbs about *is* dancing. If you want to get to know people turn the music off and talk.
ROBERT. Yes. Ha. (*Moving* L *of her*) Young people are accused of all sorts of things, but at least you don't use dancing as an excuse for a crafty cuddle like people used to. (*He gives her her drink as he closes in on her*)
MARION. You sound just like my father.

(ROBERT *looks as though he's been kicked between the eyes. He pulls himself together*)

ROBERT. Thank you. (*He goes and sits in his own chair*)
MARION. Oh, I've upset you.
ROBERT. No.
MARION. You're offended.
ROBERT. No, I'm sure it was true.
MARION. But you're still offended.
ROBERT (*smiling*) I'm not, I tell you. (*He picks up his glass*)
MARION. Then why have you gone back there?
ROBERT. Because—it's more comfortable here.

(*She snorts again*)

And I can see you. You're very nice to look at.
MARION (*pulling a face and sticking her tongue out as though being sick*) Blurgh.
ROBERT. Stunning is the word that springs to mind.
MARION. Ha.
(*She looks at her watch again. So does he at his*)
ROBERT. Have you got to get home?
MARION. Why?
ROBERT. You keep looking at your watch.
MARION. I'm timing you.
ROBERT. Ah. (*He laughs good-naturedly. It dies in his throat as he realizes. He freezes*) Timing me!
MARION. Well, you didn't bring me back here to look at me.
ROBERT. *You* brought *me*.
MARION. Oh, you poor old thing. In a minute you'll be shouting "Rape".
ROBERT. Only if you give me cause.
MARION. You're quite Olde Worlde really, aren't you? When you saw me snogging with Brian in the kitchen your face was a picture. A dirty one, too. Then when you got me back here it took you nine minutes thirty two seconds to make a remark that was even *remotely* connected with sex.
ROBERT. What's that got to do with it?
MARION. There's always a bit of chat about sex before the actual pass. I suppose it's to get you in the mood.
ROBERT. To get *who* in the mood?
MARION. The girl. You're already in it. That's why you mentioned about me snogging with Brian. To jog my sexual memory.
ROBERT. Go on.
MARION (*rising and stubbing out her cigarette*) Then having actually got something out about sex—you came and sat next to me. That only took twenty seconds. So I made things easy for you by spilling the drink. (*She perches on the R arm of the sofa*) You felt confident then. In fact, you were so confident you had to have a little laugh to let off a bit of steam. You thought you were home and dry, so I decided to make that remark about you sounding like my father. Ha. It worked a treat. Flergh. (*She gestures like a balloon collapsing, then falls into the sofa*) But you came back with a compliment. That's not bad. Oh, you did pay me a compliment earlier, but I decided not to count it.
ROBERT. Why?
MARION. Fancy saying: "Marion is a very beautiful name." That's going too far. I should drop that line if I were you.
ROBERT. Should I?
MARION. Yes.
ROBERT. Thank you.
MARION. Mind you, I suppose you're a special case. Most of the fellers I know would have made a grab as soon as we walked through

the door. They're too lazy to chat you up. They go around wearing jeans and all the tight gear, and you're expected to have a good look at the goods and make up your own mind. But you—not having a great deal to actually display, if you see what I mean,—have to bring me home, prove you're loaded, then drop some big hints about *who* you are so that I'm going to be all impressed and rush back to my girl friends and say: "Hey fellers, guess who did *me* the big favour last night".

ROBERT (*after a pause*) You don't even like me, do you?
MARION. I don't know you.
ROBERT. I mean, you don't like the look of me.

(*She shrugs non-committally*)

MARION. You're no chicken, are you?
ROBERT. Then why did you come with me?
MARION. Why did *you*?
ROBERT. I *did* like the look of you.
MARION. Fancied me, you mean.
ROBERT. Same thing, different language.
MARION. I suppose.
ROBERT. So, why did you?
MARION. Because you were the most unlikely one there.
ROBERT. I see. And if I were to make a pass at you now, what would your reaction be?
MARION. Ha. Now you're really playing it safe. You want to know the result before you've placed your bet. What do you reckon the odds are?
ROBERT. You have a remarkably precise use of words for one so young.
MARION. Oh, I'm quite bright.
ROBERT. May I ask you a question without getting a question in reply?
MARION. Depends.
ROBERT. Why did you say just now that you wanted to *keep* one up on me for a bit longer.
MARION. Supply and demand, I suppose. When something's in demand it's a sellers' market. The person who's got it is one up. I'm in demand and until I supply I'm one up.
ROBERT. And "for a bit longer".
MARION (*shrugs*) Well, the final result is never in much doubt really, is it?

(*There is a pause, then* ROBERT *laughs again*)

You know, you want to watch that little laugh. It's a dead giveaway.
ROBERT. I don't think I could cross that bit of floor between us any more than climb Everest.
MARION. Don't worry, you'll manage, sooner or later.

ROBERT. You're so cold-blooded.
MARION. What about you?
ROBERT (*indignant*) Me? I was being thoroughly circumspect.
MARION. Do you want to marry me?
ROBERT. Eh?
MARION. Do you?
ROBERT. No.
MARION. Of course you don't. Do you want to pay for it?
ROBERT. Pay for—good God, are you . . .
MARION. No. I'm just establishing. You don't want commitments and you're too stingy to pay . . .
ROBERT (*rises, moves up* L *then turns*) It's not a question of stinginess . . .
MARION. All right, put it another way. You'd think it was an insult to your virility if you had to pay. So here you are. You're on to a good thing, no complications and no cost. If that's not cold-blooded, what is?
ROBERT. Nonsense. Your whole argument implies a sort of sexual bartering that doesn't exist any more.
MARION. Since when?
ROBERT. We're not here to try to extract from each other the highest possible price for any exchange of—er—trust or intimacies that may develop as we get to know each other better. We're just two reasonably grown up, more or less intelligent people who thought it might be a good idea to spend some time together.

(*She pulls her fingers over her lower lip, making a bubbling noise*)

MARION. What a load of old codswallop.
ROBERT. I mean it.
MARION. You're great, aren't you. Have you been going round saying things like that for long?
ROBERT. Your attitude negates the whole fun of being male and female. The whole—artifice of flirtation and love play and the final pleasure that is mutually attained is something that both parties share in roughly equal amounts. Some people hold, in fact, that the female gets more pleasure out of . . .
MARION. You mean I'd enjoy you as much as you would me?
ROBERT. Probably more.

(*She looks at him from head to foot, trying not to laugh. He gets his glass, moves to the divider and puts it on the drinks tray*)

Granted you're prettier than I am, but that's beside the point. A man—a mature man—has something richer to offer than mere good looks.

(MARION *roars with laughter*)

MARION (*putting her glass on the coffee-table*) That's fabulous. I like the appeal to my old-fashioned feminine instincts best. Greater love hath no woman than that she lay down herself for her neighbour. And greater love hath not that neighbour than to oblige her, then —call her a taxi. You don't call that cold-blooded?

(*He stares at her for a while*)

ROBERT. How old are you?
MARION. Nineteen.
ROBERT (*moving down L of the sofa*) Good God.
MARION. How old are you?
ROBERT (*picking up the cigarette-box from the divider*) Cigarette?

(*He hands her one and as he is about to light it he is caught by her steady gaze. He bends and kisses her gently*)

MARION. You managed Everest.
ROBERT (*lighting her cigarette*) That was affectionate respect. (*He sits L of her*)
MARION. I'll bet you've done it so often, even you believe it now. What chance would I stand?
ROBERT. You can look after yourself.
MARION. Can I?
ROBERT. Yes.

(*She just stares at him. He looks back at her, then kisses her slowly, then passionately. Acquiescing, she just stares past him at the ceiling. She is silently crying. He comes up for air and notices this. He wipes a tear from her face*)

I'm sorry. I . . .

(*She puts her cigarette out in her glass, then puts her arms round his neck, pulling him down on top of her. In the kiss she is so overcome by sobs that he climbs off her. They move apart. She is trying to control herself; he is bored. He glances at her impatiently*)

MARION. You know that party?
ROBERT. Yes.
MARION. It was *my* party.
ROBERT. Yours?
MARION. Well, I live there, so you could call it that.
ROBERT. Well, never mind.
MARION. You know the feller on the drums.
ROBERT. The one who's not very good.
MARION. He used to be better.
ROBERT. The lino-layer.
MARION. Only part-time.
ROBERT. Well?
MARION. His name's Jimmy.
ROBERT. Good heavens.
MARION. It was his party, too.
ROBERT. You mean, you and he are living together?
MARION. Were.

ROBERT. Were?
MARION. I've left him.
ROBERT. Just now, you mean?

(ROBERT's *boredom changes to icy politeness as he sees the trap*)

MARION. Yes. I don't want to see him again.
ROBERT. I see. So you have nowhere to go in the morning.
MARION. No.
ROBERT (*after a pause; charmingly*) What about your family?
MARION. Kingston.
ROBERT. Well, there you are. I'll give you breakfast, then you can hop on a Green Line and . . .
MARION. Kingston, Jamaica.
ROBERT. Oh.
MARION. Can I stay here for a few days? Till I find a place?
ROBERT. No, I'm, afraid you can't.
MARION. I don't mind if you want to have me. I understand.
ROBERT. Thank you. That's the most beguiling invitation I've ever had.
MARION. Don't you want to, then?
ROBERT (*looking at her*) Yes. Very much.
MARION (*moving to him*) Well?

(*He moves to her*)

Then I *can* stay here for a bit.

(*There is a pause, then he pats her reassuringly*)

ROBERT. Let's worry about where you're going to stay in the morning, shall we?
MARION. Thank you.

(*She leans against him, crying, as much from relief as anything. He holds her, and quite enjoys comforting her*)

You know—I used to go with a friend of Jimmy's called Mark, who suddenly was horrible to me—and Jimmy got me to leave Mark and live with him. And lately Jimmy's been nasty—and Brian was kissing me in the kitchen when you saw us and trying to get me to go off with him—Brian is Jimmy's friend—and I asked him, and he said Jimmy had asked him to—take me over, get me out of the way because of Julie. She's Brian's girl, only Jimmy's got her now—and that's how Jimmy got me. They were all passing me round. Like a tray of cakes—have a nibble—then pass it on. It's not very nice—being passed round. (*She sobs*)

ROBERT (*smoothly*) Never mind. You've finished with them now.

(*He tries to kiss her. She sniffs and wipes her nose with the back of her hand, nearly sticking her finger in his eye. He gives her his handkerchief, then he rises, goes into the bedroom, flicks off the coverlet and turns on the light. He returns*)

There now. Anything I can get you? Cocoa? Cyanide for your boyfriend?
MARION (*smiling*) You're sweet. Thank you.
ROBERT (*sitting L of her*) Yes, you're with me now. (*His arms goes round her*) That's much better, isn't it.
(*Her smile fades*)
MARION. I suppose so.
ROBERT. Of course it is.
(*He kisses her again, removing a shoe. As he gets interested the kiss lengthens*)
MARION (*at length*) Where's your loo?
ROBERT (*pointing off L*) Through there. (*He kisses her again, removing his second shoe*)
MARION (*rising and moving above the sofa*) You'll soon be past the point of no return, so I'd better go now.
ROBERT. No one could accuse you of over-romanticism, could they?
MARION (*pausing L*) Well, what do you want?
ROBERT (*rising and moving R of her*) Don't you think you might look faintly interested?
MARION. Oh blimey, have I got to enjoy it, too?
ROBERT. That is the object of the exercise.
MARION. Please. Do you mind if I skip the ecstasy bit this time?
ROBERT (*still smoothly smiling*) We'll see. (*He picks her up and carries her to the bedroom. He lays her on the bed*) There. That's more comfortable, isn't it?
MARION. Here, you're not kinky or anything, are you?
ROBERT. Why do you ask?
MARION. This bed's red-hot. (*She jumps off the bed*)
ROBERT. Eh?
MARION. You feel it.

(*He feels the sheets and switches off the electric blanket*)

ROBERT. Oh, yes. It's the electric blanket. The daily must have flicked the switch on when she was making it this morning. (*He flaps the sheets vigorously*)

(MARION *returns to the living-room*)

It'll cool down. What are you doing back there?
MARION (*moving R of the sofa and sitting on the arm*) Look, I know I sort of threw myself at you, but—
ROBERT (*moving above the sofa to R of her*) That's all right. I'm used to it.
MARION. It's just that I don't want to disappoint you.
ROBERT. Don't worry. You won't disappoint me. And I'm willing to bet I won't disappoint you.

MARION. I wouldn't put your shirt on it.
ROBERT. I would. And more. (*He starts to pick her up*)
MARION. Hey, that's an idea. We'll toss for it. Heads I enjoy it, tails we scrub round it altogether. (*She runs R to pick up her handbag*)
ROBERT (*taking her bag and throwing it on the sofa*) We'll do nothing of the sort.
MARION. Ah, come on. All or nothing. That's fair enough.
ROBERT. If you can enjoy it after we've spun a coin, you can before.
MARION. I could, but I won't. So come on. You said you'd bet.
ROBERT. That was a figure of speech.
MARION. Coward. It's a fair gamble.
ROBERT. Fair? I have everything to lose and nothing to gain.
MARION (*very aware*) You have got something to gain. I promise you.

(*There is a pause. They stare at each other. He laughs, then stops himself*)

ROBERT (*taking out a coin*) All right. We toss. Heads, mutual pleasure, tails you sleep there (*He gestures to the bed*) and I'll sleep in the spare room. (*He points up R*) Is that sporting enough for you?
MARION. Yep. (*She crosses to the step by the bedroom*)
ROBERT. You know, they did this in a film once. Only that gamble was heads she gave in, tails they got married first.
MARION. No, thanks. I lose either way, don't I?
ROBERT. That film was made in nineteen thirty-three. The stakes are different now.
MARION. When? You're joking.
ROBERT (*annoyed*) I saw it last year at the National Film Theatre.
MARION. Oh. Go on then. Toss.

(*He tosses the coin tensely, catching it*)

Stop. Do it again. Let it fall to the ground, then there's no fiddling.
ROBERT. Do you think I'd fiddle a bet of honour?
MARION. Well, I wouldn't call this that.

(ROBERT *hesitates, then tosses. It falls between them. They both look down. They both look up at each other. They both move to the bedroom. He pulls his pyjamas from under the pillow*)

ROBERT. Good night.
MARION. Good night.

ROBERT *moves to spare room up R as* MARION *kicks off her shoes, and*

—*the* CURTAIN *falls*

ACT II

Scene—*The same. The following morning.*

When the Curtain *rises, the screens before the kitchen are still drawn. The living-room is full of smoke.* Marion *is frying eggs and laying the table. The kettle is boiling and the toast is burning. She is searching noisily for things she needs in the kitchen, without much success.* Robert *enters from the spare room in dressing-gown and pyjamas. He stops dead in his tracks at the smell from the kitchen.*

Marion. Good morning.
Robert. Good morning. A lot of activity.
Marion. I'm getting your breakfast.
Robert. Is that what it is.
Marion. Only I can't find anything.
Robert. What?
Marion. Just about anything.
Robert (*opening the screens*) If you'll just give me a minute I'll show you where things are. (*He opens the kitchen window*) It is a bit stuffy this morning, isn't it? Be a hot day, I think.
Marion. I'm sorry about the smoke, but if I could find things I need I wouldn't keep burning every piece of—oh . . . (*She runs to the grill and removes some smoking toast*)
Robert. What do you think is the decent thing to do with that? Quiet burial or scatter the ashes?
Marion. It'll be all right if I scrape it.
Robert. Burial, I think.
Marion (*putting the grill pan back and cutting some more bread to toast*) I'll do some more.
Robert (*picking up the frying-pan*) What's this?
Marion. Bacon, eggs and fried bread.
Robert. Good heavens, so it is.
Marion. Don't you like bacon and eggs?
Robert. Frankly, I forget.
Marion. I couldn't find any cornflakes or anything, either. Or do you like porridge?
Robert. If there's a blizzard and a howling north-easter . . .
Marion. It's supposed to build you up.
Robert. I spend a fortune every year trying to build myself down.
Marion. Put it back, It's getting cold.
Robert (*putting the pan back on the stove*) I think the kindest thing to do would be to let it congeal in peace. (*He moves into the hall*)
Marion. What can I get you, then? Something else?

ROBERT. No, no. Just relax and let me come to for a moment. (*He picks up the house phone on the wall*)
MARION (*moving to the hall*) But I could get something while you're doing that.
ROBERT. Please. Don't come the little woman act. (*Into the phone*) Ah, John, would you pop out and get my beigels, please . . . No, I'll need four this morning. (*He laughs*) Thank you. (*He rings off*) Let's go mad this morning and not have bacon and eggs.
MARION. All right. Do you prefer coffee or tea? I've already made coffee.
ROBERT (*crossing L towards the bedroom*) Never mind. It'll keep.
MARION. Oh, blast. You do have tea.
ROBERT. Don't make any now, I . . .
MARION (*going into the kitchen*) But I'd love to.
ROBERT. No, really. In a minute, I'll come and . . .
MARION. Oh, let me at least make some tea. I would have before, but I could only find Chinese. (*She switches off the coffee*)
ROBERT. China.
MARION. What?
ROBERT. China tea. Not Chinese.
MARION. Well, I couldn't find any Indian. Or is it India?

(ROBERT *picks up a glossy magazine from the divider and indicates the sofa*)

ROBERT (*patiently*) Just arrange yourself elegantly on that and flick nonchalantly through the pages of a woman's magazine, while I get dressed. (*He throws the magazine on the sofa*)
MARION (*moving R of the sofa*) I was only trying to be useful.
ROBERT. Ah. I'm sorry. (*Going to the bedroom*) Well, you haven't made your bed. You can make yourself useful doing that.
MARION (*following*) Ooh, thanks.

(ROBERT *goes off to the bathroom while* MARION *perfunctorily flicks the bedclothes into place. She discovers a glove which she hides under the pillow. She then arranges herself grotesquely on the sofa and flicks through the magazine. Suddenly her attention is arrested. She stares at the magazine, thinks, then gets up and looks quickly round the living-room. She goes to the bookshelf and finds some recipe books stacked together. She takes one*)

Hey.
ROBERT. Did you call?
MARION (*putting the magazine on the back of the sofa*) What did you say your name was last night?
ROBERT. Robert Danvers.

(ROBERT *enters, smirking and holding an aftershave spray*)

Ah, ha-ha. I see you've found out. Yes, I am Robert Danvers.
MARION. Is that all you do? Just *eat* for a living?

ROBERT. And drink, cook, create, write, buy wines and food, teach, criticize, review, appear on television, travel—I'm off to France tomorrow for the wine tastings.
MARION (*putting the book on top of the magazine*) You go all the way to France to taste wine?
ROBERT. Further sometimes.
MARION (*impressed*) Cor. What a super job.
ROBERT. Yes, it is, rather.

(ROBERT *exits* L, *sailing off and squirting himself with aftershave.* MARION *goes to the kitchen and looks at the cooling mess in the frying-pan and ruefully scrapes it out into the waste-bin. It is not appetizing.* JOHN *enters the corridor and rings the doorbell. He carries a bag of beigels*)

MARION. Hey, your doorbell rang.
ROBERT (*off*) It'll be the beigels. Answer it, will you?

(MARION *opens the hall door*)

JOHN. Ah, morning miss. Lovely morning.
MARION. Yes, Super.
JOHN (*innocently*) Slept well, I hope?

(*There is a pause. She stares at him, hard. He nods amicably back*)

MARION. Fine, thank you.
JOHN. He all right, is he?
MARION. I think so.
JOHN. Think so, eh?

(*He laughs. She does not*)

Here's his beigels. (*He gives her the bag*) He usually pays today. Seven and four. (*He starts to enter*)
MARION. Hang on. (*She pushes the door closed in his face*)
JOHN. Here, watch out. I . . .

(*She searches in her bag on the sofa, and takes out four pennies*)

MARION (*calling to Robert*) Have you got any money?
ROBERT (*off*) What?
MARION. For the man. Seven and four.
ROBERT (*off*) Oh, yes. Just coming.

(ROBERT *enters* L)

(*Taking a ten-shilling note from the* R *bedside drawer*) Morning, John. . . Where is he?
MARION (*nodding at the hall door*) In the passage.
ROBERT. You can't leave him out there. He's practically the family retainer.
MARION (*snorts*) Big deal. (*She goes to the kitchen*)

(ROBERT *opens the door*)

JOHN. Ah, morning sir.
ROBERT. Morning, John. How much is it? (*He gives John the note*)

(JOHN *takes the note, pockets it, then stares Robert out*)

JOHN. Seven and four, sir. It's been a quiet week.
ROBERT (*gives up*) Keep the change.
JOHN. Thank you, sir.
ROBERT. Where are the beigels?
JOHN. The young lady's got them, sir. Still warm from the oven. Lovely and fresh, sir. Enjoy your breakfast.
MARION. Porter, just before you go, I wonder if you'd do a little something for me.
JOHN (*smirking*) If I can, miss.

(MARION *brings the waste-bin into which she emptied the bacon and eggs*)

MARION. Empty this.
JOHN. Eh?
MARION. And inside you'll see some fat that's got stuck there. It's getting cold. It'll come off if you give it a good scrub with hot water before it hardens.

ROBERT ⎱
JOHN   ⎰ *together* ⎧ Oh, I don't think that's quite John's . . .
MARION ⎱   ⎨ It's not my job to clean out any old . . .
                    ⎩ (*pushing John out*) Just drop it back any time within the next half an hour or so. Ring the bell and I'll come and check it over. (*Sweetly*) Thank you so much. 'Bye (*She closes the hall door*)
ROBERT. What, in heaven's name, was all that about?
MARION. That'll teach him.

(ROBERT *and* MARION *go into the kitchen*)

ROBERT. Eh?
JOHN (*in the corridor*) What a cowson. Ceugh. Getting her bleeding breakfast. I know what I'd get her . . .

(JOHN *exits* R)

MARION (*taking the beigels from the bag and putting them on the table*) Does he always do that? Bring up the shopping and leer?
ROBERT (*taking out the ice bucket and napkin*) Don't tell me you're getting an attack of conventionalism.
MARION (*screwing up the paper bag*) I don't like being labelled by some people's assumptions.
ROBERT (*taking ice-cubes from the fridge and leaving them under the tap*) Has righteous indignation given you an appetite?

MARION. What can I do? Anything? (*She throws the paper bag at him*)
ROBERT. Just relax, sit down, and tell me the story of your life. (*He laughs*) You know, I once said that to a female and she did. My God.
MARION (*sitting R of the kitchen table*) Serves you right for seducing her. Generally the girl's expected to give in and listen to his life story as well.

(ROBERT *takes a bottle of champagne from the wine rack*)

Cor, champagne for breakfast. Are you an alcoholic? You might have told me you were a cook before you let me muck up breakfast.
ROBERT (*emptying the ice-cubes into the bucket*) I tried to last night.
MARION. No, you didn't. You tried to tell me you were famous. That's different.
ROBERT (*putting the champagne in the bucket*) You should have listened, anyway.
MARION. Huh. You sound just like . . .
ROBERT (*putting a plate in the warmer*) Don't tell me I sound like your father. It worked beautifully once, but not again.
MARION. Clever dick.

(*He laughs*)

You're pleased with yourself this morning. Did you go out and get another woman last night?
ROBERT (*putting the pan on the stove*) And don't try to shock me, either.
MARION (*peering through a beigel*) Why are these rolls called beigels?
ROBERT (*taking a bowl from the cupboard to the table*) It's a Yiddish word derived from the German. It means 'a little bend or curve'.
MARION. Do you know all about foreign foods and everything?
ROBERT (*taking two eggs from the fridge*) Well, I've eaten in most of the best restaurants of the world, but there's a lot to know.
MARION (*jabbing his waistline*) You've been bringing your work home with you. Her, her.
ROBERT. You know, you have a great deal of wit for one so young.

(ROBERT *breaks two eggs one handedly with great panache*)

MARION. Cor. The bloke in the window of our Wimpy bar does that.
ROBERT (*putting the shells on the drainer and wiping his hands*) Now, listen, you've got some serious thinking to do.
MARION. Oh, no. (*She goes into the sitting-room and lies on the sofa*)
ROBERT (*putting herbs in the mixture*) Where are you going to live?
MARION (*shrugs*) Dunno.
ROBERT. Only I'm off tomorrow. To France.
MARION. Then this place'll be all empty, will it?

ROBERT. Yes— (*He catches himself*) —and locked up.
MARION. That's criminal. A super flat like this.
ROBERT (*putting oil in the pan*) Perhaps. Meanwhile you must find somewhere to live, immediately. Tomorrow is Sunday.
MARION. You wouldn't have any ideas, would you?
ROBERT. I'm afraid not.

(MARION *is about to speak.* ROBERT *continues quickly*)

What about the West Indies?
MARION. Eh?
ROBERT (*seasoning the mixture*) Your family. Kingston, Jamaica.

(MARION *giggles*)

Wasn't that true?
MARION. No. Kingston-on-Thames.
ROBERT. Why on earth lie about it?
MARION. Why not? Kingston—ergh!
ROBERT. Well, you'd better go home.
MARION. That's out.
ROBERT. Why? A row?
MARION. No. It's just out.
ROBERT. I see. (*Moving into the living-room and above the sofa*) Will you do me a favour?
MARION. What?
ROBERT. If you answer a question with a question again, I'll hit you.
MARION (*ducking*) What with?
ROBERT (*getting out two champagne glasses from the divider and returning to the kitchen*) Will you let me give you some money so that you don't have to go back to that drummer. (*He replaces the salt and pepper on the unit*)
MARION. I don't want any.
ROBERT. All right, let me lend you some. You don't have any, do you?
MARION. No.
ROBERT (*beating the eggs*) Well, then. You'll have to borrow off someone, why not me? Then you can stay at a hotel for a night or two while you find yourself a room. Do you have a job?
MARION. Yes.
ROBERT. What?
MARION. Coffee bar.
ROBERT (*putting the eggs in the pan*) Oh, really. Give it up. Get yourself a proper job. What would you like to do? (*He puts the bowl in the sink*)
MARION (*shrugs*) Dunno.
ROBERT. Don't you care?
MARION. Not much.
ROBERT. Well, you should do.

MARION. Why should I?
ROBERT. You've got to live.
MARION. I get by.
ROBERT. You're wasting your life, your youth. If you've got some capital use it, don't fritter it.
MARION. Well, I reckon my best capital assets are my looks, so I suppose I should become a tart.
ROBERT. Don't be silly. (*He cooks the omelette*)
MARION. What's silly? If I go to bed with someone for nothing, that's wasting my capital assets. I might as well get paid doing a job I enjoy. Like you. Yeah, I'll become a connoisseur—of men. And I'll classify them. They could do with a bit of sorting out the roughs from the smoothies. When you go to Bournemouth spend the night with the only five star man in the town. Fred Blenkinsop, twenty-five Jubilee Walk. He's only a simple little grocer, but you'll be amused at his audacity.
ROBERT (*putting the omelette on the warmed plate* L *on the table*) Here, your omelette is ready. Come and eat it.

(MARION *rises, goes to the kitchen, sits* R *of the table and eats*)

MARION. Aren't you having one?
ROBERT. No. I'm having my usual.
MARION. What's that?
ROBERT (*opening the champagne*) Champagne, beigels and caviar.
MARION. Caviar? Oh, yeah. I suppose you do need a bit of help at your age. I say, could I ask you a favour?
ROBERT (*guardedly*) What?
MARION. I need my things from Jimmy's and I can't face him on my own.
ROBERT (*pouring champagne into the glasses*) You want me to go with you?
MARION. Yes, please.
ROBERT. What's he like?
MARION. It's all right. He's only violent on the drums.
ROBERT. What?
MARION. Don't worry. If he comes it, I'll bash him.
ROBERT. Thank you.

(CLARE *enters the corridor and rings the bell*)

Ah. My glittering waste-bin. (*He goes to the hall*) Don't you want to inspect it?

(ROBERT *opens the door.* CLARE *enters*)

CLARE (*crossing* L, *dropping her handbag on the sofa as she passes*) Hello, darling. I'm sorry to bother you so early. Are you most frightfully busy? But I discovered I'd left—one—of—my gloves . . . (*She sees Marion and stares, furious*)

(MARION *continues eating. There is a silence*)

ROBERT. Marion, this is Clare Dorlaton-Finch. Clare, this is Marion— (*He realizes he doesn't know her surname*)— Marion.

(MARION *lifts a hand in greeting.* CLARE *looks at Robert accusingly*) (*Disbelieving*) You came back for a glove, Clare? (*He closes the hall door*)

CLARE. Yes.

ROBERT. I see. (*He looks vaguely on the chair down* R, *the divider, and the hall cupboard*)

(MARION *eats, embarrassed*)

CLARE (*perching on the* L *arm, of the sofa and removing her gloves*) Have you known Robert long, Miss—hm?

MARION (*looking at her watch*) Ten hours.

CLARE. How nice. Practically related.

MARION (*to Robert*) Look, is she your bird?

CLARE. His what?

ROBERT. No, no, no. Clare's engaged. (*Standing on the hall step*) To someone else. Are you?

CLARE. For nearly eleven hours. (*She shows her ring*) Do you like it?

MARION (*rising*) Would you like a drink? Celebration.

CLARE. That's sweet of you, I'd love one. Ah, I see you're being given the full treatment. Shampoo and all.

MARION (*whispering to Robert*) Where are the glasses?

CLARE (*rising and going to the cupboard in the divider for a glass*) Don't worry. I know where everything is.

MARION. Oh? Is this the standard breakfast, then?

CLARE (*taking the glass to Marion in the kitchen*) Brunch, really. When the bloom wears off you get up to yesterday's rolls and instant coffee.

(MARION *pours out champagne*)

ROBERT. Clare, I simply gave Marion a bed for the night, that's all.

CLARE. Just the one night. Ships that pass.

ROBERT. I know it sounds feeble.

CLARE. And no one could accuse you of being that, could they Robert? My glove.

(ROBERT *crosses* L *and looks in the armchair*)

MARION. I'm sorry if you think I'm treading on your territory or something. (*She moves* R *of Clare*)

CLARE. Please. You're not trespassing a bit. There's a public right of way, as far as he's concerned. (*Moving down* C) You know, a sort of bridle path. Not more than three abreast. (*She sits* C *on the sofa*)

ACT II THERE'S A GIRL IN MY SOUP

(ROBERT *sighs and goes into the bedroom to look for the glove*)

MARION (*quietly*) Look, I know you're engaged, but do you want me to go?
CLARE. My dear girl, why?
MARION (*moves to* R *of sofa*) Well, I'm on your side.
CLARE. How cosy. Here's mud in your eye. (*To Robert*) And in yours, darling. Both of them.

(ROBERT *exits to the bathroom*)

MARION. Only I don't want him. You can have him.
CLARE. Thank you so much.
MARION. I mean, he's quite nice, but he's a bit wet for me—
CLARE. Wet? Robert?
MARION. —and I think you're both terrifically well suited.
CLARE. Thank you.
MARION. I mean, class and age and—oh, you know.
CLARE. No, I'm not sure that I do.
MARION (*upset*) It's just that I understand.
CLARE (*putting her glass on the coffee-table*) And I'd rather you didn't understand if you could possibly manage it!

(ROBERT *returns from the bathroom*)

ROBERT. Your glove is nowhere in this flat, Clare. Now, if you will excuse . . .
CLARE (*rising*) It's all right. I'm just off. (*She moves* L *to Robert*) Send it on. Your little Miss Thing had better be trotting along, too. You don't want her to get the sack, do you?
MARION. It's all right. (*She goes into the kitchen*) I've got an arrangement with my boss. Him and Robert take me in turns. (*She sits as before*)
CLARE. How tiring. (*To Robert*) See that your little friend doesn't exhaust herself for both your sakes. (*Going to the hall*) Good-bye, Miss–er—Enjoy your champagne. I'm sure you've had to work jolly hard for it. (*She opens the door*)
MARION. Robert, say good-bye to your mum for me, would you?
ROBERT. Please. You mustn't fight over me like this. I'm not worth it.

(MARION *giggles and* CLARE *laughs*)

CLARE. Hear that? We mustn't fight this thing. It's smaller than both of us.

(CLARE *exits.* ROBERT *closes the door*)

MARION. See that? (*She waggles the fingers on her left hand*) Pure compressed milk-bottle tops.
ROBERT. Please. (*Going to the kitchen*) I'm sorry. (*He drinks his champagne*)

MARION. I didn't think birds like that went in for flashing their engagement rings.
ROBERT. It's a habit that knows no social boundaries.
MARION. Anyway, when did you two break up?
ROBERT. Yesterday. (*He moves to the living-room*)
MARION. Wow. She didn't waste much time, did she?
ROBERT. She had him standing by. First reserve. (*He moves to the bedroom*)
MARION. Poor sucker. If you want that glove, it's under your pillow.
ROBERT. What?
MARION. I found it in the bed and put it there for a giggle.
ROBERT. Very humorous. Why didn't you say?
MARION. It would have got so complicated. Think of the explanations.
ROBERT. You're probably right.
MARION. Here, there's one thing I'm dying to know.
ROBERT. What?
MARION. Why was she wearing gloves in bed?

(ROBERT *smiles to himself and exits to the bathroom.* MARION *takes a bite from an apple. She glances at it, having bitten, and makes a noise of disgust. She picks from her mouth the piece she bit off and examines it*)

Ergh. Ah, oh, ooegh.

(MARION *gargles with champagne. She picks up a knife and flicks the maggot off the apple on to her plate. She holds the knife above her head poised as* ROBERT *enters, dressed*)

ROBERT. What are you playing at?
MARION. That apple had a maggot in it.
ROBERT (*crossing* R) Oh, put it down the sink for God's sake.
MARION. Look. Ole. A la lanterne. A bas les aristos (*She chops it in half with relish*)

(ROBERT *turns green*)

Isn't it funny the way both halves still wriggle.
ROBERT. You're a savage.
MARION. Eh?
ROBERT. A homicidal maniac. (*He goes into the kitchen*) Chopping up inoffensive maggots.
MARION. I don't call that inoffensive. It's revolting. I nearly swallowed it.
ROBERT. Well, that's not his fault.
MARION. How do you know it was a he?
ROBERT. Come on. (*He goes to the sitting-room*) We're going out.
MARION. Where to?
ROBERT. To find you a hotel. (*He picks up her bag and goes to the hall*)

MARION. What, right now?
ROBERT. Yes, now.
MARION. Don't you want me to come back?
ROBERT. No. And bring your things. (*He opens the hall door*) I don't want someone asking why you were wearing a coat in my cupboard. Come on.

(MARION *takes her coat from the cupboard*)

MARION (*at her most charming*) It's sweet of you to let me stay. Do you know, I've never been out with anyone famous before. Do you get recognized much?
ROBERT (*ushering her out*) Oh well, you know, quite often. Sometimes it all gets a bit . . .

(MARION *and* ROBERT *exit down the corridor. The* LIGHTS *fade to a Black-out*)

(*The* LIGHTS *fade up after a moment. The flat is empty.* MARION *enters* R, *using Robert's key in the hall door, She is furious.* ROBERT *follows, carrying two suitcases.* MARION *dumps her coat and bag on the* R *end of the settee and walks to and fro below the sofa*)

MARION. Isn't Jimmy vile, eh? Doesn't he make you sick? Big-headed, fat-bottomed, red-eyed, slobby—oh, I loathe him!

(JOHN *staggers along the corridor, carrying a heavy, large trunk*)

ROBERT. John, put it down in the spare room.
JOHN (*moving up* R) Put it down. I should think so.

(JOHN *puts the trunk in the spare room, and returns.* ROBERT *puts the suitcases down in the hall*)

MARION. I hope he gets her in the club and she gets him up the aisle. Then he'll be lumbered! Boy, think what their children'll look like. Gargoyles. (*She sits and helps herself to a cigarette*)
JOHN (*entering the hall*) Phew. What's in there, sir? Iron bars?
ROBERT. Books, I think.
JOHN. Oh, books, fancy.
MARION (*shouting*) Yes, you must have heard of 'em. They're for reading.

(JOHN *looks at her, shocked and frightened at the insult*)

Oh, sorry. Take no notice.
ROBERT. Here, John. Thank you.

(ROBERT *tips John a note*)

JOHN. Thank you, sir. Will the young lady be staying long, sir?
ROBERT. No, no. Purely temporary.
JOHN. I see. Fast reader, is she?

(JOHN *exits.* ROBERT *takes out the key and closes the door*)

MARION. I never noticed how ugly Jimmy looks till this morning.
ROBERT (*putting the book and magazine back on the shelves*) If I had been through that party from end to end and then had you waking me by pouring a bucket of water all over the bed I don't think that even I'd look too good.
MARION. And he stank.
ROBERT (*putting Marion's bag on the divider*) I think it was mostly the debris that smelt, not him. You could have opened the window without actually throwing the bucket through it. (*He puts Marion's coat on the suitcases*)
MARION. And what about her? Whee, what a hag. Yeah, and her roots need re-colouring, did you see?
ROBERT. I didn't notice in the mêlée. (*He goes into the kitchen and tidies up generally*)
MARION. I'm barely out of the way and she's in there. Bang. She must have been hard up. (*She laughs*) Yeah, I'll bet that bucket of water made them think, too. They were out of that bed like traps one and two, Stamford Bridge.
ROBERT. You found yourself someone else pretty quickly, too, you know.
MARION. Are you on his side or something?

(JOHN *enters the corridor carrying the waste-bin and leading Jimmy.* JIMMY *has a terrible headache and hangover. Every movement is agony for him*).

JOHN. She's in here. D'you see? *In here.* Number seven. And I hope you get her out. Give her this from me and tell her she can eat out of it now, with my compliments. (*He dumps the clean waste-bin into Jimmy's inert arms and exits*)

(JIMMY *rings the doorbell and winces at the noise*)

MARION (*awed*) Oh, no, that'll be him. (*She rises and moves to the hall*)
ROBERT. Impossible.
MARION. I'll bet he followed us.
ROBERT. John would never have given him my flat number.
MARION. Anyway, I don't want to see him.

(MARION *goes into the spare room.* ROBERT *opens the door.* JIMMY *falls in*)

ROBERT. Oh. Yes?
JIMMY. I come to see her.
ROBERT. Oh.
JIMMY. It's all right. There'll be no bother. Just a chat.
ROBERT. I'm afraid she doesn't want to see you.

ACT II   THERE'S A GIRL IN MY SOUP

(JIMMY *holds out a piece of paper.* ROBERT *looks at it*)
JIMMY. This is your address, i'n it?
ROBERT. Yes.
JIMMY. Well, I mean that's her writing. She left it behind. If that doesn't mean she wants to see me . . .
ROBERT. Yes. Well, wait here a moment. (*He opens the spare-room door*)
JIMMY. Ta. (*He moves down* RC *and sits on the chair*)
    (MARION *enters*)
MARION (*moving* L *of Jimmy*) Buzz off. Go on. I don't want to see you.
    (ROBERT *shuts the hall door*)
JIMMY. Don't start shouting, please. (*To Robert*) You wouldn't have an aspirin, would you?
ROBERT (*moving* R *of Jimmy*) An aspirin. Er—yes.
MARION. Don't give him one. Serves him right.
JIMMY. Coffee, then. Anything.
ROBERT. Yes. (*He starts to move to the kitchen*)
MARION. No. (*She pushes Robert who trips on the hall step*)
JIMMY. Hey, I thought I saw you with Brian last night?
MARION (*moving to* L *of Jimmy*) Did you?
JIMMY. I thought you went off with him.
MARION. Did you?
JIMMY. Where d'you spend the night?
MARION. Where did you?
JIMMY (*points at Robert*) Were you with him?
ROBERT (*coming into the room*) Now, just a . . .
MARION. Who were you with?
JIMMY. Oh, don't start that stupid question bit, for God's sake.
    (ROBERT *moves above the sofa*)
MARION. Why not?
JIMMY. I've been worried about you.
MARION. Worried! You rotten liar! (*She grabs a cushion from the sofa and hits him, hard*) Pretending you give a damn. Brian told me. He told me that you were trying to get rid of . . . (*She throws cushion down*)
JIMMY. I want you to stay.
MARION. Liar. (*She grabs another cushion and hits him again*) You want me out, so that you can get her in. (*She throws the cushion down*)
JIMMY (*pained*) I can't stand it. My head.
MARION (*shouting*) My head.
JIMMY. Please don't shout.
MARION. Shout! I'll scream. I'll . . .

    (MARION *picks up an ornament from the divider to throw.* JIMMY *ducks*)

ROBERT. No, not that. (*He grabs it from her, and replaces it*)
JIMMY (*nearly in tears*) Oh, my head.
MARION (*running to the bedroom*) And as for your head, I hope your head breaks open and your brains spill out on the floor and you tread on them and fall over.

(MARION *runs off to the bathroom. There is a pause.* ROBERT *smiles at Jimmy briefly*)

ROBERT. Gruesome turn of phrase, hasn't she?
JIMMY. Do you think I could have that aspirin now, please?
ROBERT. Yes, of course. (*He notices that Jimmy is still clutching the waste-bin*) Er, excuse me, but where did you get that?
JIMMY (*vaguely*) Some bloke gave it to me.
ROBERT. Thank you. (*He takes the bin and goes to the kitchen to replace it and to get a glass of water and an aspirin*)
JIMMY. My eyes feel like two piss holes in the snow. Have you got a cigarette on you?
ROBERT. What?
JIMMY. A cig—Oh, never mind. I don't think I could taste it, anyhow. (*Puts his tongue out*) Oh! I think I could grow mushrooms on my tongue. What about women, eh? I mean, I don't want to be hard, but she's a nut case.

(ROBERT *returns with the water and aspirin and moves* L *of Jimmy*)

Sometimes she's fabulous. Then you say something and she breaks up the joint. I mean, you never know where you are.

(ROBERT *moves to Jimmy, holding out the aspirin.* JIMMY *peers at him*)

Are you the one I asked for an aspirin? (*It is under his nose. He focuses*) Oh, ta. (*He swallows it and sips from the glass*) Ergh. What is that?
ROBERT. Water.
JIMMY. Blimey. (*He returns the glass to Robert*) And she does the most stupid things. Really stupid. Still, I suppose she's pretty clever really—for a bird. For instance. Birds are always saying: 'You only want me for one thing'. Always. Not just to me.
ROBERT (*placing the glass on the coffee-table*) Yes, I know.
JIMMY. What, you, too?
ROBERT. I'm afraid so. (*He takes a cigarette and lights it*)
JIMMY. Yeah. Everyone I know. All over the world at any given moment there must be millions of birds saying: 'You only want me for one thing'. It's like the Luton Girls' Choir in fifty languages. D'you know what I say?
ROBERT. What? (*He sits* L *on the sofa*)
JIMMY. I say 'What else have you got to offer?' That floors 'em. But when I met her—(*Gestures after Marion*)—we're sitting there, necking, and she's feeling a bit fruity, you know, and I says to her, joking: 'You only want me for one thing.' And she says to me:

ACT II   THERE'S A GIRL IN MY SOUP   39

'What else have you got to offer?' And d'you know I couldn't think of anything to say. (*Aggrieved*) And now, just because I'm moving Julie in, she goes screaming blue murder.

ROBERT. It's only natural, isn't it?

JIMMY (*picking up the cushions and wincing*) Natural? (*Rising*) Why? Julie'd be company for her. (*He sits very close to Robert with a hand resting on Robert's leg*)

(ROBERT *tries to get up*)

With two of 'em to look after me they can cut the housework in half. They'd be laughing. But no, that's too reasonable for her—oh,—blinking women! If I didn't fancy 'em so much I'd change sides, I think.

(ROBERT *struggles up quickly and moves* L *of the sofa.* JIMMY *places the cushions on the sofa and leans thankfully back on to them. There is a pause*)

ROBERT. Excuse me. Are you going to have a nap or are you going to get her out of here?

JIMMY. I want to, don't I, but look at her. She gives me your address and then yells at me the whole time.

ROBERT. She's upset.

JIMMY. Upset? Her? What about me? I'm humiliated.

ROBERT. Do you expect her to enjoy sharing you?

JIMMY. Why not? Most of the blokes I know are having it away with different birds all over the place.

ROBERT. Well?

JIMMY. Well, I just want to get mine all under the one roof and save myself a bloody fortune.

(MARION *enters and moves* L *of Robert*)

MARION. All right. It's all over. Out.

(ROBERT *edges slowly above the sofa to* R *of it*)

JIMMY. Look, come back, Mari. You'll like Julie. She's a good kid.

MARION (*to Robert*) Isn't he a charmer?

JIMMY. Don't you want to know about Brian, then? He's dead keen.

MARION. Stuff Brian.

JIMMY. What are you going to do then?

MARION (*perching on the* L *arm of the sofa*) I should have thought that was quite obvious.

(MARION *throws a kiss to* ROBERT, *who moves into the hall*)

JIMMY. Ah, now look here, Mari. I'll help you find a room; you've got to go somewhere.

ROBERT. I wish you'd both go somewhere. (*He opens the hall door*) Anywhere.

(JIMMY *rises and moves to the hall.* MARION *moves ahead of him*)

JIMMY. There. See the sort of bloke he is? He won't look after you. One night, then out.
ROBERT. That's right. Out.
MARION (*joining Robert*) Yeah, out.
JIMMY. I just don't want to leave you here with him.
ROBERT. What is so offensive about her staying with me?
JIMMY. Well, I mean—don't you think you ought to know better at your age? I mean she's not the sort of kid to go tarting off with—with a . . .
ROBERT. With a what?
JIMMY (*to Marion*) Let's talk outside. (*He goes into the corridor*) Please, Mari.

(MARION *follows Jimmy, pulling the door to.* ROBERT *goes into the kitchen to make coffee*)

Please, Mari, come back.
MARION. What, with her there? Get knotted.

(JIMMY *moves away* R)

Er. What was the party like after I left?
JIMMY. Oh. It dropped dead on its feet about five; some comedian pulled the plug out of the bath.
MARION. Oh, Shame.
JIMMY. Look, you're only staying with him to have a go at me, aren't you? I don't know how you can stand that old git touching you after me. All that old flesh. Ergh. It gives me the willies.
MARION. Well he's terrific. Better than you.
JIMMY (*touching her gently*) Ah, Mari. Come back. Think of the fabulous times I give yer.
MARION (*bursting out*) Don't. Don't touch me. Go and touch her instead.

(ROBERT *opens the door*)

ROBERT (*shouting*) Stop this shouting. There are other people living in these flats, too, you know. (*He slams the door, and looks at himself in the hall mirror*)
MARION. You'd better go.
JIMMY. He's a bit choked, i'n he? It's not his fault, I suppose. He can't help it. I'd better say I'm sorry. (*Calling*) Hey, I say, mate.

(ROBERT *moves to the door as* JIMMY *pushes it open. It hits* ROBERT *full in the eye. He staggers back with a cry of pain, and sits on the edge of the divider*)

What's that?
MARION. What happened?
JIMMY (*moving into the flat*) Are you all right?

ACT II THERE'S A GIRL IN MY SOUP 41

(MARION *goes into the kitchen and soaks a napkin*)
ROBERT. Get out, you clumsy, bloody twit.
JIMMY. What have I done?
MARION. Here, this'll help.
ROBERT. Get out.
JIMMY. I only came to say I'm sorry.
MARION. Go and sit down. Help him, Jimmy.
JIMMY. Come on, this way. (*He takes Robert's arm*)
ROBERT. I'm quite capable of walking, thank you. (*He moves away from Jimmy and trips down the step from the hall. He sits on the sofa*)
MARION (*coming from the kitchen and applying the napkin*) Here, put this on.
ROBERT. Ow. Careful.
MARION. I was.
ROBERT. It hurts.
MARION. I'll do it again if you don't shut up.
ROBERT. It's cold.
MARION. It's good for you.
JIMMY (*moving above the sofa to* C) You know what you want. A dirty big steak.
ROBERT. I don't keep dirty big steaks.
MARION (*sitting on the* R *arm of the sofa*) Put it back. (*Stroking his head*) There.
ROBERT. It's swelling up, I think.
MARION. It'll be all right in a moment. (*She gives him a little peck*)
JIMMY. Here, cut it out.
MARION. What?
JIMMY. All that bit. I don't like it.
MARION. Then don't watch. (*She puts her arms round Robert*) I thought you were going.
JIMMY. Honestly, I don't know how you can do it.
ROBERT. Do what?
JIMMY. Well, I mean. Making up to an old bloke, like him.
MARION. I bet you never thought you'd drive me to this.

(ROBERT *jumps up*. MARION *falls into the sofa*)

ROBERT. That's enough. Out. (*He goes to the hall and opens the door*)
MARION. Yeah, clear off.
ROBERT. You are the most arrogant young idiot I've ever met. You imagine that if a woman looks at you it must be love and that anyone over fort— thirty-five must be repellent.
JIMMY (*going into the hall*) Well, let's face it. Chicks don't go out with old blokes like you for their lovely profiles, do they?
MARION (*rising*) Go on. Out. (*She moves to the hall*)
ROBERT. I could beat you to any woman.
JIMMY. You what?
ROBERT. Just because I don't have the nappy marks on me.

JIMMY. Look, mate, the only sort of marks you've got are . . .
MARION (*pushing Jimmy*) Out, I said.

(JIMMY *staggers from the force of the push and his head snaps back. He freezes, clutching his head in his hands*)

JIMMY (*at length*) Oh, my God. I thought it'd come off.
MARION (*pushing Jimmy outside*) Go on. Go back to your girlfriend.

(MARION *closes the door and* JIMMY *shambles away and exits* R. MARION *stalks up and down the hall*)

ROBERT (*crossing* L *above the sofa*) What a specimen! Horrible urk. What did you say he was? A lino-layer? (*He sits* L *on the sofa*)
MARION. Only part-time.
ROBERT. It's too good for him.
MARION (*perching on the back of the chair down* R) Did you see that? He was really jealous. Dead choked.
ROBERT. Why on earth did you give him my address?
MARION. I'd never thought he gave a damn. It was always me.
ROBERT. He only thinks of you as a bird, a chick, an invention you take to bed and it does the washing up. Still, I suppose he's young.
MARION. Young? He's twenty-three, the oldest man I ever—Yeah, he is young, bit childish really. And he's worried, saying those things about you to put me off. (*She stares at Robert speculatively, then rises, moves to the sofa and kneels on it*) Excuse me, (*She touches his cheeks, then pinches them*)
ROBERT. Careful.
MARION, Sorry. (*She puts her hands under his jacket and feels his ribs*) Mmm. Not bad. Quite nice, in fact. A bit beefy. Still.
ROBERT. Are you thinking of buying me for slaughter?
MARION. You smell nice, too. That's important. He thinks it's pouffy to use aftershave.
ROBERT. Oh, he shaves, does he?

(*She kisses him. It develops. They break*)

MARION (*thoughtfully*) Yeh, smashing. (*sitting back*) I don't know what he's on about. You kiss jolly well.

(ROBERT *preens himself*)

ROBERT. There has been the occasional female in my life who hasn't found me repulsive. My God, but you're lovely.
MARION. My God, but you're corny.
ROBERT. But I meant it. You're sweet and fresh, like—like peeled lychees.
MARION. Oh, blimey. Still, you've had a lousy time, haven't you? All this trouble and a smack in the eye and not even a sniff of the barmaid's apron.

ACT II   THERE'S A GIRL IN MY SOUP

ROBERT. Well, whose fault is that, may I ask?
MARION. Not yours.
ROBERT. Precisely.

(*They look at each other for a moment*)

MARION (*kneeling up*) Okay, then.
ROBERT. Okay, what?
MARION. I'm game if you are.
ROBERT. What, now?
MARION. Yes, right now.
ROBERT. You're just trying to get even with that zombie.
MARION. What's the matter? Scared?
ROBERT (*laughing*) Me? Scared?
MARION. Yeah. Do you need some of your caviar first?
ROBERT (*outraged*) I don't need any . . .
MARION. Then why make Jimmy an excuse.
ROBERT. He's not my excuse, he's yours. But don't worry, I'll soon convert you.

(*He picks her up and takes her to the bedroom*)

MARION. You're always carrying me off to bed.
ROBERT. Fun, though, isn't it?
MARION. If you like those old silent films.

(*He puts her on the bed and straightens up, wincing slightly and breathing hard*)

ROBERT (*easing off his shoes*) I do. I love them. (*He lies beside her*)

(*They embrace.* ROBERT's *hand moves on her back, searching for a zip or buttons*)

MARION. Hey, if you're going to cover me with passion while you try to undress me, save it. It's easier if I do it myself. (*She rises and stands below the bed undressing*)

ROBERT (*taking off his jacket*) You're determined to keep everything matter of fact, aren't you? Never mind, we'll see. (*He starts to remove and fold up his trousers*)

MARION. Rolling about trying to get out of your clothes is all right in theory, but it doesn't work in practice.

ROBERT. Theory, practice. Where did you learn to make love? In a laboratory?

MARION. No, worse luck. A laboratory would have been warmer. (*She runs into the living-room*)

ROBERT. Now, where are you off to?
MARION. Cigarettes, for after.
ROBERT. Oh, yes.
MARION (*picking up the box on the coffee-table*) Your box is empty.
ROBERT. Does it matter at this moment?

MARION (*going to the divider and checking the box on it*) Yes. Haven't you got any?
ROBERT. I'll find you some in a minute.
(*He goes to the living-room without his trousers. She goes to bedroom*)
MARION. And bring the champagne. Be fun.
ROBERT (*moving above the sofa*) You wouldn't like me to go out for a walk? Then you can have your bean-feast in peace. (*He takes a packet of cigarettes from the drinks cupboard*)
MARION. I'm just making everything nice.
ROBERT (*moving round R of the sofa*) It's very thoughtful of you, and you're an eminently practical young lady, but you are destroying all —(*He comes into full view*)—the mystery that should surround the sexual intimacies. Why don't you try being a little romantic for a change? (*He moves to the coffee-table, undoing the packet*)
MARION. Romantic!
ROBERT. Yes. (*Moving to the chair L*) Look beyond the factual to —something else.
MARION (*laughing*) Look beyond the factual. (*She becomes helpless with laughter*)
ROBERT. May I share the joke?
MARION. Say that again and look in the mirror.
ROBERT. I was merely saying that you should look beyond . . . (*He realizes what a buffoon he looks, drops the cigarettes, goes for his trousers and hauls them on, crossing R below the sofa*)
MARION. Oh, have you changed your mind? (*She does up her dress, still laughing*)
  (ROBERT *is furious and mortified*)
ROBERT. I fail to see that the sight of a man without his trousers need cause you such hysteria.
MARION. I'm sorry, but you just looked so funny.
ROBERT. To hell with what I looked like.
MARION. Don't shout, it makes your eye look livid . . .
ROBERT (*moving L above the sofa*) I ought to put you across my knee.
MARION. Try it. You take one step towards me and I'll burst out laughing.
ROBERT. Go away. (*He goes into the bedroom*)
MARION (*sparring*) Coward, come on. (*Moving C below the sofa*) I'll tie one hand behind my back.
ROBERT (*putting on his shoes*) I think you actually enjoy all this.
MARION. I'll say. Half a puff of pot and I'm away.
ROBERT. Well, I don't.
MARION (*moving up L*) Can't you stand the pace?
ROBERT. No.
MARION (*Flopping down across the back of the sofa*) Middle-aged Romeos should lay off young girls if they can't stand the pace.

(*There is a pause*)

ROBERT (*furious*) I think you'd better go.
MARION. Eh!
ROBERT (*taking money from the* R *bedside drawer*) I'll give you some money for a hotel. Here. (*He moves* LC)

(*There is a pause*)

MARION. You really mean it? You want me to go?
ROBERT. Passionately.
MARION. Oh. (*After a pause, she rises, picks up her bag and goes to the hall*) Well, thank you for putting me up. I have enjoyed it. I hope you have. (*She puts her coat round her shoulders. After a pause*) Would you like me to wash up first?
ROBERT. A woman comes in.
MARION (*picking up her cases*) Oh. (*She stands holding her cases, looking forlorn*)
ROBERT. Orphan Annie. Your range is remarkable.

(*She suddenly drops her cases and runs to him, throwing her arms about him. He is taken aback. She is crying*)

What is it?
MARION. I love you.
ROBERT. You love me so you hurl insults at me.
MARION. That's why. If I didn't, I wouldn't.
ROBERT. Oh, come off it. (*He moves to the bedroom*) If you didn't you wouldn't. (*He puts on his jacket*)
MARION (*following him*) But I do.
ROBERT. Do you want this money?
MARION. No, thank you. (*Pause*) Do you want to try again?
ROBERT (*crossing her and moving* R *below the sofa*) No, thank you. (*He sits* R *on the sofa*)

(*She sits gingerly on sofa. She smiles appealingly at him*)

Sunshine through rain.
MARION. Eh?
ROBERT. First the tears, then the brave little smile.
MARION. I feel brave with you.
ROBERT. My God, but you're lov—Um.
MARION. Oh. Go on. Say it, please.
ROBERT. You are. Very lovely.
MARION. And so are you, you're—(*Searching*)—very nice. And handsome. (*She kisses him*)

(ROBERT *does not respond*)

Aren't you going to take advantage of me now I've fallen for you?

(*She moves to the bedroom*) I should, if I were you. Best time to. (*She slips out of her dress*) Don't worry. I promise I won't laugh. I'll look the other way. (*She holds out her hand to him*)

Like a lamb to the slaughter, ROBERT *rises and starts to move towards her, as—*

the CURTAIN *falls*

ACT III

SCENE—*The same. Two weeks later.*

When the CURTAIN *rises, the telephone is ringing.* ROBERT *enters into the corridor in a hurry.* MARION *follows him, loaded down with all the oddments that one acquires on a holiday abroad and the flight back. She has a straw beach bag and a B.E.A. bag. In them are brandy, cigarettes, fruit, cigars, a long French loaf, a Beatles-type yachting cap, sandals, beach ball, hotal ashtrays and towel.* MARION *also has a large, daft hat. She is in a very chic dress bought in France, and* ROBERT *is in lightweight clothes.* ROBERT *opens the front door and runs across to the telephone. As he reaches it, it stops ringing.* MARION *stands in the hall, half submerged in bits and pieces.*

ROBERT. Blast.

(ROBERT *searches in his pockets for a card.* MARION *drops everything*) Careful, darling, you'll break something.

(ROBERT *exits to the spare room.* MARION *dumps the things on the sofa*)

MARION. Isn't it stinking to be back. Stink, stink, stink, pooh.

(ROBERT *returns from the spare room with an invitation card*)

ROBERT. Oh hell, it is at twelve-thirty. I'm going to be late. Try that number for me, darling. (*He moves to the bedroom*)
MARION. Don't go. Eh?
ROBERT. I must.
MARION. We could say the plane was held up even longer. Then we could go out somewhere.
ROBERT. Where?
MARION. The park. The river. Battersea Funfair.
ROBERT. No, thank you. (*He opens the screen*)
MARION. Well, somewhere.
ROBERT. Look, darling, these people are opening a restaurant on top of a vast skyscraper and without me there they'll lose a lot of publicity.
MARION (*taking off her hat and moving to the bedroom*) Bighead.
ROBERT. It's true. If I don't go nobody'll even know they're up there. They'll all probably die of exposure.

(ROBERT *exits to the bathroom.* MARION *sits* R *on the bed and dials a number on the telephone*)

MARION (*into the receiver*) Je veux s'il vous plait, le numero un et un, seven and six . . . 'Allo, 'allo is zat ze crows' nest? . . . O.K., buster, there's going to be a raid on your crumby joint. I've got the D.A. wants to speak to you. (*She covers the mouthpiece and calls sweetly*) I've got 'em.

(ROBERT *enters and takes the phone from her*)

ROBERT. Thank you. (*Into the receiver*) Hullo. Robert Danvers here . . . I beg your pardon? (*To Marion*) They've rung off. (*He replaces the receiver*)

MARION. It must be the wrong number.

ROBERT. Try it again. Imagine telling me to do a thing like that.

(ROBERT *exits* L. MARION *dials again*)

MARION (*in a "posh" voice*) Hullo. Hullo. Is that the crows' nest? . . . I have a call for you from Mr Robert Danvers. Hold on, would you, please. (*She covers the mouthpiece and shouts*) Hey, pudden, I've got 'em again. (*She moves* L *of the stool*)

(ROBERT *enters*)

ROBERT. Did you cover the mouthpiece then?
MARION. Yes, why?
ROBERT. We don't want anyone else to hear that name, do we?
MARION. Don't we?
ROBERT (*sitting on the bed*) No.

(MARION *goes to the hall, chanting* "Georgie, Porgie, pudden and pie . . .")

(*Into the receiver*) Hallo. May I speak to Victor Hilary, please. Robert Danvers here . . . Thank you.

(MARION *starts rummaging in the B.E.A. bag. She extracts several large cartons of cigarettes*)

(*To Marion*) How on earth did you have the nerve to bring all those through the customs.

MARION. I didn't. You did. I put them in your bag.

ROBERT. What! (*Into the telephone*) Hullo, Victor. Robert here. I'm terribly sorry. We've only just got back and I'm going to be late. We stayed on an extra week in Cannes, then got held up at Nice Airport last night . . .

(MARION *puts on the yachting cap, then goes into the bedroom and takes off her coat*)

We? We, the passengers. *I* stayed on . . .

(MARION *holds up a warning finger*)

I don't know, some mechanical fault.

(MARION *puts the cap on Robert*)

It's all so damned inefficient.

(MARION *stretches out on the bed*)

They say the plane won't go and there are all these other planes— (*He notices Marion*)—lolling about all over the airport. Now they've lost two of my cases. I can't be with you till one. . . .

(MARION *signals*)

Oh, good. Hang on. (*He covers the mouthpiece. To Marion*) Yes?
MARION. Ask him if I can come, too.
ROBERT (*into the telephone*) It's all right. I'll see you soon. Goodbye. (*He rings off*)
MARION. Why can't I go? (*She rises, goes to the living-room and puts the cigarette cartons in the drinks cabinet*)
ROBERT. You'd be bored stiff.
MARION. I will be here.
ROBERT. I can't just take you along to a serious occasion that's all been arranged in advance.
MARION. Wasn't the wine-tasting serious?
ROBERT. That was different.
MARION. Yeah, no press there.
ROBERT. It's not that.
MARION (*picking up the beach ball*) That's why you disowned me at London airport, wasn't it?
ROBERT (*moving above the sofa*) I'm only thinking of you.
MARION. You don't have to worry. I'm not ashamed of you.
ROBERT. Ashamed? My dear girl, do you realize how many women would give their eye teeth to be in your shoes?

(JOHN *enters the corridor with two cases and rings the doorbell*)

Answer that, please.

(MARION *throws the ball.* ROBERT *catches it and exits to the bathroom.* MARION *opens the door*)

MARION (*rudely*) Oh, hullo.
JOHN (*disappointed*) Oh, hullo. (*Crossing to the bedroom*) Mr Danvers's cases. Shall I take 'em through?

(JOHN *goes to the bedroom.* ROBERT *enters*)

MARION. Yeah. (*She takes two ashtrays from the bag and puts them on the coffee-table*)

JOHN (*warmly*) Oh, hullo, sir. Nice trip, I hope.
ROBERT. Splendid, thank you, John.
JOHN. Good. Nice to see you back. Both of you.

(MARION *puts two other ashtrays on the divider*)

ROBERT. John. There are two more cases coming from the air terminal when they find 'em. Pay the taxi and bring 'em up when they arrive, would you?

(MARION *rummages in her handbag*)
JOHN. Right, sir.
ROBERT. Thank you. Here. (*He tips John*)
JOHN. Thank you, sir. (*He goes into the living-room*)

(ROBERT *exits into the bathroom*)

JOHN. Anything I can do for you, miss?
MARION. Such as?
JOHN. Like getting you a taxi.
MARION. No, thank you, porter. (*She deliberately waves her handkerchief in the air. It is full of scraps of confetti*)

(JOHN *stares appalled as he is showered with confetti*)

I'm not going anywhere. (*She takes a pair of scissors from her bag*)
JOHN. Yes, miss—er—madam. Oh.

(JOHN *exits* R *miserably.* MARION *picks up a hotel towel, sits on the sofa, and starts picking at it.* ROBERT *enters from the bathroom*)

ROBERT. I must be off now. Really, darling. All that junk you brought back.
MARION. It's lovely. Reminds me.
ROBERT (*picking up an ashtray from the coffee-table*) What's this?
MARION. An ashtray.
ROBERT. The Carlton? Did you steal it?
MARION. Oh, they expect it. Anyway, I liked them.
ROBERT. Them?
MARION. I've got a towel, too.
ROBERT. You'll be arrested.
MARION. It's all right. I'm picking the name off.
ROBERT. This lunch will go on rather, so I'll see you at about half-past five. (*He kisses her, then goes to the hall*)
MARION. Some lunch! Hey, pudden.
ROBERT. I think "Robert", now we're back, don't you?
MARION. I've had a terrific time, Robert. Thank you.
ROBERT (*moving back to her*) The pleasure was mutual. (*He kisses her*) You look adorable.
MARION. You're improving. You almost sounded as if you meant it.

(ROBERT *exits down the corridor. The* LIGHTS *fade to a Black-out.*
The LIGHTS *fade up after a moment.* MARION *wearing an apron, is standing above the kitchen table pouring wine over some peaches in a bowl.*
ANDREW *enters the corridor and rings the bell.* MARION *opens the door*)

Yes?

(ANDREW *looks at her for a while*)

Well? Can I help you?

ANDREW (*sadly*) I think it's too late.
MARION. What? What do you mean?
ANDREW. Is himself in?
MARION. No. Why?
ANDREW. Ah. Is he due?
MARION. Sort of. Why?
ANDREW. Would it be inconvenient if I waited?
MARION. I don't know. What do you think?
ANDREW. Hm. That depends, doesn't it? Is that something cooking I can smell?
MARION (*anxiously*) Does it smell all right?
ANDREW. Fine. Are you cooking it?
MARION. Yes.
ANDREW. And is he expecting you to be here? Cooking?
MARION. Yes, then no. Is he expecting you?
ANDREW. You mean "yes" to your being here and "no" to your cooking, I take it.
MARION. It's a surprise. Do you think it's silly of me?
ANDREW. Well, it's courageous.
MARION. Yeah, well, I thought I should have a go. Dinner for two. Does this mean it's for three?
ANDREW. I wish it did, but I'm afraid I have to get home. Just ask him to give me a ring, would you, please, when he feels strong enough to lift the telephone? My name is Andrew.
MARION (*amazed*) Andrew. You're Andrew? *You're* Andrew. Andrew Hunter, the editor.
ANDREW. Yes, but don't be too impressed. It's a very lowly station, really.
MARION. Come in.
ANDREW. Thank you. You, I take it, are Marion.

(MARION *lets him in and closes the door.* ANDREW *stands by the sofa*)

MARION. So you're Andrew? (*She stares at him for a while, then lets out a dirty giggle*) Her-Her.

(ANDREW *shifts uncomfortably, then inadvertently checks his flies*)

ANDREW. Tell me. Have you ever thought of becoming a dentist's receptionist?
MARION. No, why?
ANDREW. You have that indefinable something. A sort of knack for making one feel unclean.
MARION (*laughing*) I'm sorry. It's just you. I mean Robert's description of you. I imagined someone quite different.
ANDREW. Not the young Apollo that you see before you.
MARION. No.
ANDREW. Robert has this thing, you see. He does this transference business. He imagines he's Dorian Gray and I'm the sort of verbal picture.

MARION. It doesn't work, does it?
ANDREW. You know, you're even prettier than I thought. Do you mind if I sit down?
MARION. No. Do. (*She clears the towel and other things off the sofa and takes them into the bedroom*)
ANDREW. Did you enjoy your trip to France? (*He sits R on the sofa*)
MARION. Yeah, it was fabulous. Mind you, I think they're all a bit cracked about this wine-tasting.
ANDREW. Yes, I know exactly what you mean.
MARION (*moving C above the sofa*) When we were in some of those wine cellars I thought we were going to have to kneel down and pray or something. But it was smashing. I got sloshed every day. (*She perches on the back of the sofa*)
ANDREW. You're supposed to spit it out so that you can judge the next lot.
MARION. Why waste it? (*Sliding her legs over the back of the sofa*) Nobody wanted my opinion.
ANDREW. Was it fun going on to Cannes?
MARION. Oh, it was great. Except for those waiters making snide remarks when Robert was out of earshot. I settled that, though. I went out and bought a wedding ring and some confetti and I got Robert to change hotels. Then, in the taxi, I pushed a bit into his trouser pocket. He was furious.
ANDREW. What happened?
MARION. When he went to tip the taxi-driver he sprayed it out all over the foyer. He went purple and I blushed and everybody from then on was as nice as pie. Have you ever tried it?
ANDREW. Only once and that was official.
MARION. It's super. I'll never go on a dirty week-end again without some. Everybody's so *nice* to you. Then Robert fell for it and overdid it like mad. Every time he went out it was like a paper chase.
ANDREW. Where's Robert now?
MARION. Opening some new restaurant. He's late. (*She slides into the sofa*) Can I ask you a personal question?
ANDREW (*winces*) What do you call personal?
MARION. Do you ever chase a bit of spare?
ANDREW. Just a splash, please, and a little ice if you have it.
MARION. Eh? Oh, a drink? (*She rises and moves to the drinks*) Sorry. Whisky? You haven't answered my question. (*She prepares his drink*)
ANDREW. Which one did you have in mind?
MARION. About chasing a bit of spare.
ANDREW. Why did you ask it?
MARION. Well, Robert and I were talking about making passes and he said you were the only married man he knew who didn't. (*She gives him his drink*)
ANDREW. He's right. Cheers!
MARION (*sitting on the back of the sofa*) Why don't you?
ANDREW. Why don't I? Well, apart from any question of love and

loyalty, I think it's such bad manners to your wife. People always find out and it's rather like picking your nose in public when you have a perfectly adequate handkerchief in your pocket.

MARION (*rising and going into the kitchen*) Robert says that's why he won't ever get married. Because he's bound to be unfaithful.

ANDREW. Who brought up marriage, you or him?

MARION. Oh, him. But I think he was just covering himself in case I did.

ANDREW. That sounds like our Robert.

(MARION *checks the time on the cooker and turns the gas on under the artichokes and new potatoes*)

MARION. Do you know anything about food?

ANDREW. Yes. I have a lifetime's experience of eating.

MARION. Do I put these peaches in wine in the fridge—or not. It says the peaches should be cold, but the wine warm. So which is best?

ANDREW (*rising and moving to the hall*) If it was me I'd shove the peaches back in the fridge, leave the wine where it is and drink it.

MARION. I think I'd better leave them. I'm doing roast lamb and artichokes to start with. I thought I couldn't go far wrong with that. What do you think?

ANDREW. Sounds fine. If he criticizes, throw it at him.

MARION. I say, are you any good at chopping mint?

ANDREW. I've no idea.

MARION (*putting the mint board on the table*) Would you like to find out?

ANDREW (*resignedly*) You know, this, my girl, is why husbands spend most of Sunday lunch-time in the pub. (*He sits* R *of the kitchen table*)

(*The telephone rings*)

MARION. I think I've got everything timed right. That's when the trouble starts. When everything's ready at once.

(MARION *answers the phone while* ANDREW *chops mint*)

(*Into the receiver*) Hallo? . . . Yes . . . Oh, hallo . . . Yes . . . That's up to you . . . What? Right now? I dunno . . . Oh. All right . . . Yes. See yer. (*She rings off and returns to the kitchen*) I have to go out.

ANDREW. Right now?

MARION. Yes. Could you keep an eye on things, please?

ANDREW. Yes, all right.

MARION (*taking off her apron*) Wear this, it'll save your suit. (*She puts her apron on him*)

ANDREW (*rising*) What do I do if anything explodes?

MARION. It won't. (*Picking up the oven glove*) Just give this joint a baste, would you? Here. Put this on (*She puts the oven glove on him*)

ANDREW. Thank you. If you can do this to me in ten minutes, what state is his lordship in?
MARION (*moving to the hall*) He's bearing up. See you.

(JOHN *enters* R, *struggling with two suitcases*)

ANDREW (*following Marion*) Yes, I hope so.

(MARION *goes and opens the door, meeting John*)

MARION. Just put them in the bedroom, porter.

(MARION *exits* R. JOHN *crosses with the cases and meets Andrew.* JOHN *eyes the apron*)

JOHN. Evening, Mr Hunter. I see you've met her.

(JOHN *takes the cases into the bedroom*)

ANDREW. Yes, she's charming, don't you think?
JOHN. Charming. Oh blimey.
ANDREW. What's up? Aren't you keen?
JOHN. I don't know. (*Crossing back to the hall*) I haven't really got to know her yet, have I?
ANDREW. Come off it, John. I won't split on you.
JOHN. Hm.
ANDREW. Only it looks as though you may be seeing quite a bit more of her.
JOHN. Yeah, I know. Well, he's had a good long run, so I suppose it's only justice, getting her. Only I get her, too, and I haven't done nothing, have I?

(JOHN *exits* R. ANDREW *pours himself another drink, then goes into the kitchen and opens the oven. He smells*)

ANDREW. Um! (*He picks up a magazine Marion was using*) A simple roast for two by Clement Freud. Clement Freud? The little traitor.

(ROBERT *enters the corridor with a bunch of flowers. He opens the hall door and enters the hall*)

ROBERT. Darling. (*He enters the living-room, leaving the door ajar*) Darling.
ANDREW. Yes, my sweet.
ROBERT. Who let you in?
ANDREW. Guess.
ROBERT. Where is she?
ANDREW. She received a phone call and rushed out. She won't be long.
ROBERT. Oh.
ANDREW. Don't worry. Andrew is watching over you. There's din-dins in the oven and if you pat my head I'll fetch your slippers. Woof-woof.

ACT III   THERE'S A GIRL IN MY SOUP

ROBERT (*putting the flowers on the divider*) Why are you wearing that thing?
ANDREW. It's hers. She passed it on to me.
ROBERT. Take it off.
ANDREW (*sitting at the table chopping mint*) Well, I must offer you my heartiest congratulations, old boy. She is a doll. This is what I call going out in a blaze of glory.
ROBERT. Going out . . . ?
ANDREW. And she cooks, too. Why she bothered with you, God knows.
ROBERT (*looking into the spare room*) She's a sweet little thing.
ANDREW. Sweet! She's like a rampant panzer division.
ROBERT. What do you mean, she cooks?
ANDREW. It's all there. I'm just the sentry.
ROBERT (*moving to the hall; sentimentally*) You mean she's trying to get me dinner. Now, isn't that just like her. What other woman would do that?
ANDREW. Just about anyone I can think of.
ROBERT (*going to the kitchen and looking in the oven*) I mean for me. Oh, my God, I hope it's edible.
ANDREW. Don't criticize, just eat it.
ROBERT. I am not criticizing. I'm deeply touched. Roast lamb. Good. Artichokes, splendid. She shouldn't leave the lid on. Makes 'em taste bitter.
ANDREW. Really? I must make a note of that.
ROBERT (*picking up the wine bottle*) Good God, she's drunk an entire bottle of my Château Gris, Nuits St Georges 'forty-seven.
ANDREW. Try the peaches.
ROBERT. Great screaming balls of fire. She's soaking 'em in it. A whole bottle.
ANDREW. Yes. Now you can get drunk over the pudding.
ROBERT. After all those years in my cellar just to be poured over . . . (*He laughs*) Oh, well, we all make mistakes. Look. Bless her. She's pushed the cork in.
ANDREW. Robert, are you sure she hasn't pushed your cork in.
ROBERT. I say, old chap, do you think she'd be offended if we disposed of this mint and made some onion sauce instead?

(ROBERT *throws away the mint and scrapes the bowl clean, watched by an indignant* ANDREW, *who finally removes his glove and apron.* ROBERT *gets out some onions*)

ANDREW (*rising*) So much for my contribution. Where on earth did you find this girl?
ROBERT. We met. She fell for me and here we are.
ANDREW. Just like that. (*He goes into the living-room*)
ROBERT. Yes.
ANDREW (*moving L above the sofa*) The poor thing took one look at

your thickening waistline, screamed with ecstasy and keeled straight over in a dead faint.
ROBERT. More or less, yes.
ANDREW. Her-hup! I don't believe a word of it.
ROBERT. It's true. Do you remember that party where we all got mixed up? She was living there.
ANDREW. No wonder she wanted to leave.
ROBERT (*moving into the living-room and pouring himself a sherry*) She was living there with a drummer. He was moving another female in. So . . .
ANDREW (*sitting in the chair* L) Any port in a storm.
ROBERT (*moving to the sofa*) I must admit that at first she saw me as an avuncular fuddy-duddy who'd look after her.
ANDREW. How does she see you now?
ROBERT (*sitting on the sofa*) I think that our trip abroad has changed the image. She's so intelligent, you know. Very witty. Incredible in one so young.
ANDREW. Must one be senile to be witty?
ROBERT (*smiling*) That's exactly what she said. She sees through things.
ANDREW. You mean that continued proximity to you enables her to realize that although the fabric is decaying the structure is still sound.
ROBERT. It's no good. You can't rile me. Not today. She's very appreciative of being with me. I teach her a lot.
ANDREW. Like cooking.
ROBERT. Yes, among other things.
ANDREW. There. Now you have something in common for the long winter evenings. Then when it's spring and you're feeling sexy, you can swop frying-pans and catch each other's pancakes.
ROBERT. There's one thing different, though.
ANDREW. Oh, what's that?
ROBERT. She teaches me a lot.

(ANDREW *looks at Robert*)

ANDREW. Ah. Now, that is different.
ROBERT (*putting his glass on the coffee-table*) I say. I must tell you. If ever you want to be treated like royalty when you go to a hotel with a woman—I had the most fabulous idea . . .

(MARION *enters the corridor*)

ANDREW. Take some confetti.
ROBERT (*blankly*) Yes, it works like a dream.

(MARION *enters the hall*)

MARION. Hallo, darling. (*To Andrew*) Did you keep an eye on things? (*She closes the door*)

ANDREW. Well, you only left thirty seconds ago. Not a lot can have happened.
MARION (*to Andrew*) Huh. (*In passing Robert, she moves to give him a peck*) How are your taste buds? Exhausted?
ROBERT. I've had a long, hard lunch.

(ROBERT *puts his face up to Marion. She recoils*)

MARION. Pheeoo! What did they feed you on? Dead cat?
ROBERT. It was very highly spiced.
MARION. I should think it needed to be. (*She goes into the kitchen to look in the oven*)

(ROBERT *breathes on to his hand, testing*)

ROBERT (*rising*) One of the hazards of my profession.
ANDREW. I didn't like to mention it.

(ROBERT *goes into the kitchen. He gets a slice of dry bread and eats it*)

ROBERT. It's sweet of you to cook, darling. I do appreciate it. But, darling, you've used a whole bottle of my Chateau Gris, Nuits St Georges 'forty-seven.
MARION. Oh, sorry. I wasn't sure, and it was the dirtiest old bottle I could find. Ask Andrew to stay and eat. He'll be company for you.
ROBERT. Aren't you company?
MARION. Ask him.
ROBERT (*moving below the kitchen table*) You do have to get back to Gilly for dinner?
ANDREW. Yes.
ROBERT. He can't.
MARION (*moving* R *of Robert*) Oh well—look—I know I've got dinner and everything, but—would you mind eating alone?
ROBERT. Not if it's absolutely necessary.
MARION. Thanks. (*She cuddles Robert*) Oh, you've got me some flowers.
ROBERT. Well, don't sound so tragic.
MARION. They're lovely.
ROBERT. I've got something else for you.
MARION. I've got a present for you, too. (*She moves into the living-room and above the sofa towards the bedroom*)
ROBERT. For me? Why?
MARION (*stopping by the entrance to the bedroom*) I thought you deserved one. Anyway, you had a birthday while we were away.
ROBERT. How do you know.
MARION. I looked in your passport.

(ROBERT *reacts and goes into the spare room.* ANDREW *laughs*)

(*Quietly*) Andrew, please stay and eat.
ANDREW. I'm sorry. My shepherd pie is waiting.

(ROBERT *enters with a package and comes down* C)

ROBERT. Here we are.
MARION (*moving* C) For me?
ROBERT. For you.
MARION. Oh, you shouldn't have.
ROBERT. Go on.
MARION. Aspreys. I don't think I should.
ROBERT. Open it.

(MARION *opens the parcel and takes out a bracelet*)

MARION. Oh, it's fabulous, super. Oh, Robert, I can't take it.
ROBERT. Let me put it on you. (*He does so*) It's the reason I was late back.
ANDREW. I wish I could afford excuses like that.
MARION (*putting the box on the sofa*) You haven't looked at yours yet.
ROBERT. I haven't got it yet.
MARION. Oh. (*She goes to the chair down* L) Excuse me, Andrew. (*She pulls a large tube from under the cushion on Andrew's chair*)

(*Playing the game*, ROBERT *closes his eyes*. MARION *puts the tube in his hand*)

ROBERT. How lovely. Thank you. (*He feels it*) What is it?

(MARION *sits* L *on the sofa*)

ANDREW. Looks like a long overdue hint to me.
MARION. It's just what he needs.
ROBERT. Toothpaste?
MARION. No. It's hormone face cream.
ROBERT (*opening his eyes*) Eh?
MARION. You rub it in on your face and it makes all your wrinkles disappear.
ROBERT. Am I supposed to rub this in at night like some bloody old hag?
MARION. No. It's no good at night, it's only temporary. It won't last till morning.
ANDREW. Ha! What happens? Does he just lie there in the small hours disintegrating like a horror film?
MARION. You can wear it if you're going out somewhere special, or if you have to be on telly. It lasts about four hours.
ANDREW. Then—blah—Frankenstein.

(ROBERT *sulks*. MARION *is upset*)

MARION. Oh, Robert.
ANDREW. Look, Marion, don't worry, he'll be creeping off for a sly rub as soon as he gets used to it.

MARION. Well, I didn't know what to get you. And I thought that would be useful.

ROBERT (*smiling with difficulty*) I'm sorry. It's a lovely present. Thank you.

(ROBERT *sits in the chair down* R. *His smile collapses. There is an embarrassed pause*)

ANDREW. Well, I think I'll creep quietly away. (*He rises*)

MARION (*panics*) No, Andrew. (*She rises and moves to* ANDREW) Please don't. I'm just . . . Please keep Robert company . . .

ROBERT (*putting the tube of cream by him in the chair*) I don't need a nanny. I'm quite capable of looking after myself while you do whatever it is you have to.

MARION. Andrew, would you like to make sure that nothing burns in the kitchen?

ANDREW. Eh? Oh, certainly. Could I have a refill first?

MARION (*moving above the sofa*) Here. Take the decanter.

ANDREW (*following Marion and taking the decanter*) Thank you. You're very beautiful when you're bossy.

ROBERT. She doesn't like compliments.

ANDREW (*amazed*) Don't you? Really?

MARION. Not much.

ANDREW (*moving below Marion to the kitchen; sadly*) I wish you'd have a word with my wife, sometime. (*He draws the kitchen screens*)

(MARION *goes to the bedroom, gesturing to* ROBERT *to follow. They sit on the end of the bed,* MARION L, ROBERT R)

MARION. I thought it was better not to tell you in front of Andrew. I'm going.

ROBERT. I see. (*He does his best not to let on how hurt he is*) What's the rush?

MARION (*with a shrug*) It has to be now. (*She rises*)

ROBERT. I suppose this couldn't last.

MARION. No. (*She takes a drawer from the chest up* L *and empties the contents on the bed*)

ROBERT. At least this is tidy. A jolly fortnight abroad, then . . .

MARION. Yes. (*She replaces the drawer, then empties and replaces the second one*)

ROBERT. Must you go right at this moment?

MARION. Yes. Sorry. Oh. (*She puts one of the cases on the stool below the bed*) I've still got my things in your case. I'll return it.

ROBERT. I was quite looking forward to seeing you tonight, too. Why don't you go tomorrow?

MARION. He's coming for me, any minute.

ROBERT. He?

MARION. Jimmy. (*During the following, she packs the things from the drawer in the case*)

ROBERT (*rising*) The drummer?
MARION. Yes.
ROBERT. *That horrible bloody drummer?*
MARION. Yes. Ssh.
ROBERT. I won't ssh. Why the hell are you . . . ?
MARION. Keep your voice down. I've just seen him. He's missed me.
ROBERT (*aghast*) *He's missed you.*
MARION. Yes. He's forgiven me.
ROBERT. Eh?
MARION. For going away with you.
ROBERT. *He's forgiven you?* Don't you remember *why* you came here?
MARION. Yes. He's got rid of her.
ROBERT. What?
MARION. Well, he's doing it now, actually. He asked me to come back. He begged me. Said she was dull. He missed the flying crockery. I said not while she was there.
ROBERT. You have your pride. (*He sits on the stool*)
MARION. Yeah. He said three would be interesting. A new experience. I said, new for him. In the end he said he'd get rid of her. (*Sentimentally*) Fancy Jimmy missing me.
ROBERT. I shall miss you.
MARION. I know. Shall I get him to send her round here?
ROBERT. No, thank you.
MARION. She's very pretty and she's got nowhere to go.
ROBERT. You said she was a hag a fortnight ago.
MARION. I was biased then. Oh, go on. You've got room. It'll be company for both of you.
ROBERT. I don't want Jimmy's cast-offs.
MARION. Don't be beastly about her.
ROBERT. This sudden magnanimity.
MARION. You wouldn't like it if someone called me one of Jimmy's cast-offs. Or one of yours.
ROBERT. I'm not casting you off. Neither did he.
MARION. Well, you wouldn't like it if someone called you one of my cast-offs. You'd be terribly insulted. I don't seem to have a clean pair of knickers to my name.
ROBERT. Why do you want to go back to that yob?
MARION. I don't know, I—Jimmy—well—he must love me after all.
ROBERT. What you mean is, you think *you* love *him.* A fortnight ago you said you loved me.
MARION. I did? So I did. (*Thoughtfully*) Isn't it funny?

(ANDREW *creeps cautiously into the living-room*)

ROBERT (*rising*) Didn't you mean it?
MARION. Yes, I did. (*She shrugs and goes into the living-room*)

(ROBERT *sits again*)

ANDREW. Oh, sorry. (*He starts for the kitchen*)
MARION (*collecting her coat and bag from the hall*) It's all right, Andrew.
ANDREW. All right? I heard shouting. Then it went quiet.
MARION. I'm sorry, Andrew. Robert's not himself for the moment.
ANDREW (*realizing that Marion is collecting her belongings*) Ah.
MARION (*putting her bag and coat on the R end of the sofa*) Yes, that's right, I'm off.
ANDREW. Ah.
MARION (*collecting the ashtrays from the divider, and the bracelet box from the sofa*) He's a bit surprised.
ANDREW. Ah.
MARION. Be all right in a minute.
ANDREW. Ah.
ROBERT. Don't keep saying 'Ah' as though you're having a medical.
ANDREW. Oh. (*He returns to the kitchen*)

(MARION *returns to the bedroom*)

ROBERT. So you only said you loved me so that I'd keep you here.
MARION (*putting the things in the case*) No, I meant it. Well, you don't love me, do you? So what's the odds?

(JIMMY *enters the corridor and rings the doorbell*)

Oh, that'll be Jimmy. He's got to go to Basingstoke for a one-night stand. The others will be waiting. Would you mind very much if I let him in and you kept out of the way.
ROBERT (*rising*) Certainly I would.

(ANDREW *comes from the kitchen*)

MARION. I tried to stop him coming here, but—

(JIMMY *rings again*)

—well, you know what he's like.
ROBERT. Only too well! And I will not have him in here.

(ANDREW *crosses* L *to the bedroom*)

MARION. Please keep your temper.

(ANDREW *knocks on the bedroom screen and pushes it open an inch*)

ANDREW. I think there's somebody at your door.
MARION. It's Jimmy. (*She moves towards the bathroom and exits*)
ANDREW. Jimmy.
ROBERT. Stuff Jimmy. (*He moves to the bathroom and exits*)

ANDREW (*to himself*) Stuff Jimmy! (*Moving to the hall*) There's still someone at your door.

(ANDREW *answers the front door*)

Ah. You must be Jimmy. Come in.

JIMMY. Eh? You're not him, are you?

ANDREW (*moving into the living-room*) Well, I'm certainly not her.

JIMMY. Eh? Oh.

ANDREW. Have a drink? Scotch?

JIMMY. Thanks. (*He closes the door*) No, I mean you're not Flyblow, what's his name, who's had Mari here.

ANDREW (*pouring a drink*) I haven't had the pleasure. Are you the one who's having her—I mean—getting her next?

JIMMY (*peeping into the kitchen*) We were together before he broke it up.

ANDREW. Ah! Yes of course. You're the drummer.

JIMMY. Yes.

ANDREW. What happened to your latest acquisition?

JIMMY (*crossing to look in bedroom*) Oh, I booted her arse out of it.

ANDREW. Did you really? You sweet old-fashioned thing.

JIMMY. Where is she then?

ANDREW. Who knows? Rubbing her arse, I presume.

JIMMY. Eh?

(*They stare at each other, puzzled*)

ANDREW. Oh, you mean Marion. (*He laughs*) She'll be out in a moment. Let her detach herself from him in her own way. (*He hands Jimmy the drink*)

JIMMY. What? (*He takes the drink and moves below Andrew to down* L) She having trouble or something?

ANDREW (*moving down* R) Could be. But you won't help. Things are a bit tacky at the moment; if you joined in they'd be irrevocably glued, I think. (*He sits in the chair* R)

JIMMY. Hm. (*He sits in the chair* L)

(MARION *returns from the bathroom with toilet things and piles them into her case. She then enters the living room*)

MARION. Oh, hallo. Andrew, please stay. He's gone all quiet.

(ROBERT *enters the bedroom*)

ANDREW. All right.

MARION (*calling Robert*) Darling—

(JIMMY *rises*)

—come and meet Jimmy. (*She moves above the sofa*)

JIMMY. Darling? (*He moves below the* L *end of the sofa*)

ACT III   THERE'S A GIRL IN MY SOUP   63

MARION. Don't be silly.

(ROBERT *enters the living-room*)

You two haven't met properly, have you. Now *please* for me. *Be friends.* Jimmy, this is Robert. Robert, Jimmy.

ANDREW. And after you've shaken, I want you to come out of your corners fighting.

JIMMY. Ha. Quite a lad, your mate, isn't he? Ah, well. Don't know why I'm getting the needle. I mean, I've got the bird. No hard feelings, eh?

ROBERT. None.

(ROBERT *and* JIMMY *shake hands.* MARION *moves* R *of the sofa*)

JIMMY. I mean you seem to have looked after her all right, and that's the main thing, I suppose.

ROBERT. I hope you'll look after her, too.

(MARION *sits on the* R *arm of the sofa*)

JIMMY. Don't worry. I'll see she gets three square jabs a day.

ROBERT. I mean it. Things like seeing she gets to bed at a reasonable . . .

JIMMY. Don't worry about that. I'll see to it.

MARION (*to Andrew*) Aren't they both sweet.

JIMMY (*slapping Robert on the back*) Come on, we should be mates. I mean, you might say we're sort of related, in a way.

ROBERT. Related?

JIMMY. Yeah. I mean . . . (*He gestures at himself, Marion and Robert*)

(ROBERT *sits down* L)

MARION. Yeah. Sort of unofficial husbands-in-law. Oh, blimey, I forgot to put the peas on. (*She rises*)

JIMMY. What?

ROBERT. I don't think it matters now.

MARION. Don't be silly; you've still got to eat, haven't you? (*She goes into the kitchen*)

(JIMMY *moves up* L)

ROBERT. Andrew, I could do with a drink.

(ANDREW *rises and moves above the sofa*)

MARION. Hey, what are these onions for?

ANDREW. That's the beginning of some onion sauce. Robert thought it would be better than mint. (*He pours out a whisky*)

(MARION *comes from the kitchen with a vase. She puts the flowers in it and stands them on the divider*)

MARION. Really. Oh, I must remember that. You know, I'm going to miss learning all these things.

JIMMY. Come on, Mari. The others are waiting outside for us in the minibus. We've got to get to Basingstoke. If they go without us we'll have to walk it. Drum kit and all.

MARION. Darling, would you get my cases, please?

(ROBERT *rises*)

ROBERT }
JIMMY } (*together*) Certainly, darling.

(JIMMY *and* ROBERT *meet on the bedroom step*)

JIMMY. Now, look here . . .

ROBERT. Sorry. (*He goes to the hall*) I'll get the porter.

(ANDREW *hands Robert his drink as he passes.* ROBERT *picks up the house phone*)

JIMMY. What for? (*He goes into the bedroom*)

(MARION *joins Jimmy in the bedroom*)

ROBERT. There's another trunk, books or something.

JIMMY. Another one! Oh, blimey!

ROBERT (*on the phone*) John, would you come up for the cases, please . . . I know you have. Now you take them down again. (*He rings off; urgently*) Andrew.

ANDREW. What?

(MARION *loads Jimmy up with her things*)

ROBERT. Get out. (*He moves* R *of the sofa*)

ANDREW. Eh?

ROBERT. The spare room. Anywhere.

ANDREW (*kindly*) Don't do it. (*Moving* L) It's too late. (*He sits down* L)

(JIMMY *and* MARION *come from the bedroom and cross to the hall*)

JIMMY. Blimey. This is going to be a comfortable ride tonight. You'll have to sit on top, Mari.

(MARION *stuffs the French loaf under Jimmy's chin*)

That's all I needed.

(JIMMY *exits down the corridor.* ROBERT *puts his glass on the coffee-table and takes* MARION'S *hand as she is about to follow Jimmy*)

ROBERT. Marion, don't go with him. Stay. I'll marry you. But please don't go.

MARION. No, I—I've got to.

ROBERT. I'll take you round the world. Anything.
MARION. You're just saying that because you think I'm throwing myself away on him.
ROBERT. No. I love you. Please stay.
MARION. Oh.
ROBERT. You will?
MARION (*tearfully*) Oh, I wish I could. You deserve to get me. But I can't.
ROBERT. But I'm offering to marry you.
MARION. Yes.
ROBERT. Good God. (*He sits on the* R *arm of the sofa*)
MARION. But thank you for asking. (*She kisses him*)

(JIMMY *enters*)

JIMMY. Here, here, what's the game?
MARION. He's just asked me to marry him?
JIMMY. Of all the dirty rotten tricks. The minute my back's turned he's nicking my bird.
ROBERT (*rising*) Will you marry her?
JIMMY. You mind your own business.
ROBERT. You see? He doesn't give a damn.

(MARION *runs* L *above the sofa. As he speaks,* JIMMY *advances on* ROBERT, *who backs down* L)

JIMMY. It's blackmail. Listen, I'm just about up to here with an old git like you taking liberties with my bird, just because I'm being civilized about the whole thing.
MARION. Shut up, Jimmy.
JIMMY (*continuing to back Robert* L) I've never cared very much for you, and I'm just about ready, now, to stick one on . . .

(MARION *gets between Robert and Jimmy, pushing them apart.* ROBERT *falls into the chair down* L. ANDREW *leaps aside just in time*)

MARION (*authoritatively*) Shut up. I'm not going to marry Robert, or you either.

(ANDREW *moves* R *above the sofa*)

JIMMY. I didn't ask you.
MARION. Don't change the subject.
JIMMY. Anyway, what's wrong with me?
MARION. There's not time at the moment.
ANDREW. Excuse me, do you mind if I put in a word?
MARION. What?
ANDREW. Well, you're obviously not going to live happily ever after with Young Lochinvar here.
JIMMY. Who?
MARION. Scrub round it.

ANDREW. And Robert isn't going to live happily ever after without you. Why don't you divide yourself up and make them both happy?
MARION. Eh?
JIMMY (*horrified*) You mean . . .? (*He gestures at Marion, Robert and himself*)

(JOHN *enters the corridor*)

ANDREW. Precisely.
JIMMY. Now, look here, you.
MARION. Shut up. (*Moving* R *above the sofa*) Go on, Andrew.

(JOHN *rings the bell*)

ANDREW. I've finished, I think. Shall I answer the door?
MARION (*sitting on the* R *arm of the sofa*) Share myself out, you mean? (*She puts her coat, hat and bag on the sofa*)
ANDREW. It sounds as generous as it is.
ROBERT. Do you think I'll make do with half a woman?
ANDREW. No. A whole woman. Half the time. Sounds like paradise to me.
MARION (*to Jimmy*) Like your idea for yourself, only the other way round.
JIMMY (*crossing quickly* R *above the sofa to face Andrew*) I think it's disgusting.(*He starts backing Andrew round the sofa*) And what's more, I'm getting a bit fed up with the ideas you and your mate have been giving her.

(ANDREW *back down* L *as* JIMMY *advances*)

JIMMY } (*together*) { She's sharp enough without your help, so just keep your . . .
ANDREW } { I'm very sorry, I had no intention of . . .

(ANDREW *backs on to Robert's foot.* ROBERT *yells with pain.* ANDREW *turns quickly to see what is wrong and his elbow catches Robert in the eye*)

ANDREW. I'm terribly sorry, I . . .
JIMMY (*laughing*) Which one's that? The good one, or the bad one?
MARION (*rising and crossing* L) Shall I get you something for that?
JIMMY (*crossing* R) Come on, you.
MARION. But he's hurt . . .
JIMMY. He's fractured his left eyelash. He'll live. Out.

(JIMMY *grabs Marion's hand.* MARION *protests, but* JIMMY *hauls her out of the flat.* MARION *grabs her coat and bag on the way.* JIMMY *and* MARION *exit down the corridor*)

ANDREW. I do apologize, I was trying to be helpful.
ROBERT. Go home to your wife.
ANDREW. Does it hurt?
ROBERT. Yes.

ANDREW. They say a piece of raw steak . . .
ROBERT (*rising*) I know what they say.
JOHN (*moving into the doorway*) Did you want me, sir?
ROBERT (*peers*) Oh, John. (*He crosses* R *below Andrew*) The trunk. But they seem to have gone without it. (*He sits on the sofa*)
JOHN. Oh, has she gone, sir?
ROBERT. Yes.
JOHN. For good?
ROBERT. I'm not sure.
JOHN. Oh.

(MARION *runs in, and grabs her hat from the sofa*)

MARION. Could you get my trunk, please?
JOHN (*eagerly*) Yes, right away.

(JOHN *goes into the spare room*)

MARION (*moving to Andrew*) Thank you for thinking of that. You're smashing. (*She kisses Andrew, then kneels* L *of Robert on the sofa, putting on her hat. To Robert*) See you, darling, soon. Oh, your poor eye.
ROBERT. Could you do that, live with him and—see me?
MARION. Well, I don't know. I've never tried it before. It might work.
ANDREW. Thousands of people find it very satisfactory.
MARION. Anyway, think what a weapon I'll have to use on him if he steps out of line.
ROBERT. Splendid. Now I'm a blunt instrument.

(JOHN *enters from the spare room with the trunk*)

JIMMY (*off*) *Mari!*
MARION. Coming. 'Bye, darling. (*She goes to the hall*) Oh, your dinner should be ready. I do hope you enjoy it.
JOHN. Sure you've got everything.
MARION. If I haven't I'll be back.
JOHN. Oh, good. I'll look forward to that.

(MARION *runs off down the corridor.* JOHN *follows her off*)

ROBERT. It's no good. I couldn't do it.
ANDREW. No—of course not. Have a drink.
ROBERT. No, thank you. My stomach feels very peculiar. Is that love, do you think?
ANDREW. No, wind. (*Sitting on the* L *arm of the sofa*) You haven't eaten yet.
ROBERT. My God, that girl. You know, I jumped out of my taxi and took a tube this afternoon."

ANDREW Good God.

ROBERT. The traffic was gridlocked.
ANDREW. It must have been.
ROBERT. There was a girl in the compartment...like Marion...same hairstyle, clothes, everything. So, I smiled at her.

(*He does so, painfully, remembering.*)
ANDREW What did she do? Scream for help?
ROBERT. NO. She smiled back...then **she** offered me her seat.

(ANDREW *stifles his laughter*)
ROBERT. It was the most shattering experience of my life.

ANDREW. Did you accept?

(*The telephone rings.* ROBERT *ignores it*)

Your telephone.
ROBERT. Huh. It'll only be some female. (*He automatically rises and goes to the bedroom to answer it, sitting on the* R *side of the bed*) Flaxman five four six eight . . . Speaking . . . Who? . . . I can't quite understand you . . . Did I? . . . Hang on, would you. (*He covers the mouthpiece. To Andrew*) Some foreign female says I asked her to have a Chinese meal with me.

ANDREW. Good idea. She might take you out of yourself.
ROBERT. I think I'm already out.
ANDREW (*rising*) Go on. Do you good. (*He moves* R, *and picks up the tube of cream*) I'll leave you to it, old friend. Just one thing. Do yourself a favour. (*He tosses the tube of cream to Robert*) Rub some well in before you meet her. Oh, and, Robert, don't stay with her longer than four hours.

(ANDREW *exits down the corridor.* ROBERT *toys with the tube of cream, opening it*)

ROBERT. Hallo, look, I don't really feel like going out this . . .

It's your only night off, eh? Well, in that case, if you feel like a quiet evening you can come round here if you like and I'll give you some roast lamb—with artichokes. (*He rings off. He looks at himself in the mirror on the table as he wipes some cream on his face. He glances at his watch*) My God, but you're lovely!

CURTAIN

FURNITURE AND PROPERTY LIST

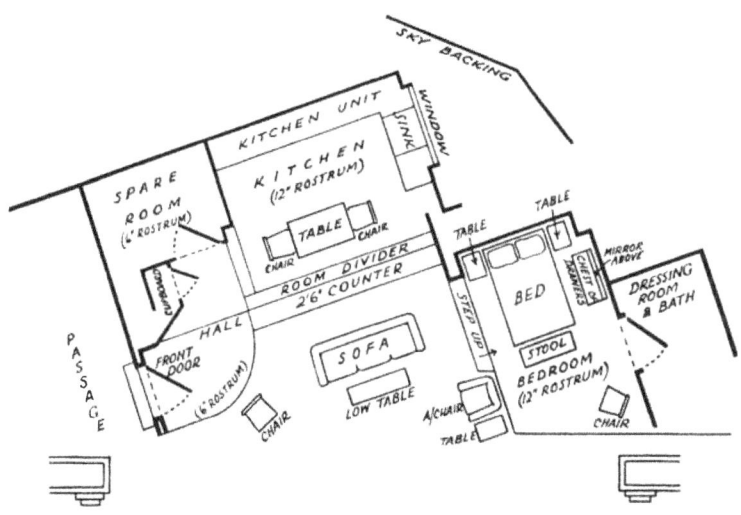

ACT I

On stage: LIVING ROOM:

>Sofa (C). *On it:* cushions
>
>Armchair (down RC). *On it:* cushions
>
>Armchair (down LC). *On it:* cushion, Clare's coat
>
>Coffee-table (C). *On it:* ashtray, cigarette-box
>
>Dividing unit comprising drinks cabinet, built-in record-player, bookshelves (up C). *On it:* drinks tray with 4 whisky glasses, soda syphon, decanters of whisky and sherry, bottle of Courvoisier, ice-bucket with cubes, record on turntable, bowl of fruit with one real apple, 3 ornaments, ashtray, lighter, books in shelves, magazines, lamp stand, clock. *In drinks cabinet:* champagne glasses, various bottles

HALL:
Hallstand. *On it:* lamp stand, ashtray, letters
Cupboard. *In it:* hooks, dressing
On wall: house phone, mirror
On door: practical bell

BEDROOM:
Bed (up LC). *On it:* bedding, Clare's bag, pyjamas under R pillow, blanket switch on floor
Bedside table (L). *On it:* lamp, Clare's glove, ashtray
Bedside table (R). *On it:* lamp, telephone. *In drawer:* ten-shilling and five-pound notes, aspirin bottle
Stool (*below bed*)
Chair (down L)
Chest-of-drawers (up L). *In it:* (top R small drawer) Robert's socks, (first drawer) Marion's underwear including 5 pairs of knickers, (second drawer) other clothes, slacks, jumpers, blouses. *On top:* mirror

KITCHEN:
Built-in wine cupboard (up C). *In it:* wine bottles in rack, 2 champagne bottles
Oven (up C)
Stove (up C). *On it:* spatula fork, ladle, oven glove hanging near
Unit (up C). *On it:* coffee percolator with coffee grains in, 3 plates, 3 knives, 3 forks, salt and pepper pots, bottle of oil, herb jars, loose herbs, electric kettle, mixer, toaster
Sink (up L). *In it:* bowl. *On draining board:* dish cloth
Fridge. *In it:* eggs, ice-cubes
Window-sill (up L). *On it:* jug of water, 2 glasses, aspirin
Wall cupboard (up C). *In it:* crockery
Small shelf. *On it:* cookery books
On wall above stove: omelette pan
On wall below wine cupboard: 3 copper saucepans with lids
In cupboard below stove: mixing-bowl, tins of food
Under sink: vegetable container with onions
In cupboard under sink: champagne bucket and napkin, waste disposal bin
In alcove L: tea towel
Table (C). *On it:* 2 plate mats, breadboard, bread and knife, small plate with slice of bread on it, ashtray
2 chairs

SPARE ROOM:
Bookstand

Off stage: Bath robe (CLARE)
Hand-mirror (CLARE)
Suit, shirt, tie, shoes (ROBERT)
Air ticket, press card, timetable (ANDREW)

Personal: ROBERT: ten shilling note
watch
keys
wallet with five-pound note and visiting-card
lighter
handkerchief
coin

MARION: watch

ANDREW: wallet with five-pound note

ACT II

Strike: Dirty glasses, plate of bread, water jug
Cigarettes from box on divider
All but 2 cigarettes from box on coffee-table
Cigarette-ends from ashtrays

Check: Marion's bag on sofa, with 4 pennies in it

Set: Hand-mirror on R bedside table
Glove under bedclothes
Packet of cigarettes in drinks cabinet
R side cabinet doors open to reveal champagne glasses
Shake champagne bottle and ease cork for quick opening
Turn on electric ring in kitchen
Put boiling water in percolator, switch on and bring to boil and make coffee, just before CURTAIN up
Pre-crack 2 eggs
Pre-grease omelette pan
Turn on smoke 3 minutes before CURTAIN up
Grill pan with burnt toast in oven
Frying-pan with eggs, bacon and fried bread on stove
Kitchen screens closed
Bedroom screens open
All doors shut

Off stage: Aftershave lotion (ROBERT)
Bag of beigels (JOHN)
Keys (MARION)
2 suitcases (ROBERT)
Trunk (JOHN)
Piece of paper (JIMMY)

Personal: CLARE: engagement ring
ROBERT: ten-shilling note

THERE'S A GIRL IN MY SOUP 73

ACT III

Strike: All dirty things from kitchen
Damp cloth and cigarette packet from coffee-table
Letters from hall stand
B.E.A. ticket from divider
Dirty glasses
Cases
Marion's coat and bag
Cigarette-ends from ashtrays

Set: Bed made
Marion's case beneath L side of bed
Marion's coat in hall cupboard
Cigarettes in both boxes
Tube of hormone cream down side of chair L
Invitation card and trunk in spare room
4 whisky glasses and one sherry glass on tray
Whisky in decanter
Cabinet doors shut
Bowl of peaches, bottle of wine, *Sunday Times Supplement* with Clement Freud recipe open, on kitchen table
Vase on window-sill
2 pans of boiling water (one with lid on) on electric rings
Joint of lamb in oven
One pan with lid on standing near rings
Check ladle, fork and oven glove
Mint board, mint and knife on unit
Bread on unit
Kitchen screens shut
Bedroom screens open
All doors shut

Off stage: French loaf, beach ball, B.E.A. bag with 4 cigarette cartons, magazines, towel with "Carlton" sewn on it, 4 hotel ashtrays, beach bag with bottle of wine, 1 cigarette carton, yachting cap (MARION)
4 suitcases (JOHN)
Bunch of flowers (ROBERT)
Gold bracelet in Asprey's box and envelope (ROBERT)
Toilet bag (MARION)

Personal: ROBERT: coins
keys
MARION: handbag with handkerchief containing confetti, small scissors

LIGHTING PLOT

Property fittings required: 4 table lamps, neon strip in kitchen.

> INTERIOR. A flat comprising living-room, hall, kitchen, bedroom, and corridor outside. The same scene throughout.
>
> THE APPARENT SOURCES OF LIGHT ARE, by day: windows in 'fourth wall' and up L in kitchen; by night, table lamps and neon strip
>
> THE MAIN ACTING AREAS are R, down RC, up C, down C, down LC, up L, I

ACT I .Evening

To open:	Effect of evening light. Fittings off	
Cue 1	ROBERT: "I must show you. . . ." *Quick fade to Black-out*	(Page 11)
Cue 2	When ready *Lights up in corridor*	(Page 11)
Cue 3	ROBERT switches on lights *Snap on fittings in hall and living-room*	(Page 11)
Cue 4	ROBERT switches on bedroom lights *Snap on bedroom lights*	(Page 22)

ACT II Morning

To open:	Effect of morning light.	
Cue 5	ROBERT: "Sometimes it gets a bit . . ." *Quick fade to Black-out*	(Page 35)
Cue 6	When ready *Fade up to opening lighting*	(Page 35)

ACT III Morning

To open:	As opening of Act II	
Cue 7	MARION: " . . . as if you meant it" *Quick fade to Black-out*	(Page 50)
Cue 8	When ready *Fade up to opening lighting*	(Page 50)

EFFECTS PLOT

ACT I

Cue 1	On CURTAIN up *Soft music on record-player*	(Page 1)
Cue 2	ROBERT turns off record-player *Music off*	(Page 3)
Cue 3	ROBERT turns on record-player *Soft music on record-player*	(Page 11)
Cue 4	MARION turns off record-player *Music off*	(Page 15)

ACT II

No cues

ACT III

Cue 5	As CURTAIN rises *Telephone rings*	(Page 47)
Cue 6	ROBERT reaches the telephone *Telephone stops*	(Page 47)
Cue 7	ANDREW: " . . . lunch-time in the pub" *Telephone rings*	(Page 53)
Cue 8	ANDREW: "I think it is of mine" *Telephone rings*	(Page 68)

MADE AND PRINTED IN GREAT BRITAIN BY
LATIMER TREND & COMPANY LTD PLYMOUTH
MADE IN ENGLAND

www.ingramcontent.com/pod-product-compliance
Ingram Content Group UK Ltd.
Pitfield, Milton Keynes, MK11 3LW, UK
UKHW021845210426
5322IPUK00022B/486